Israel and
the Palestinians

ISRAEL AND THE PALESTINIANS
Israeli Policy Options

Edited by
Mark A. Heller and
Rosemary Hollis

 **CHATHAM HOUSE**

Published in Great Britain in 2005
by the Royal Institute of International Affairs,
Chatham House, 10 St James's Square, London SW1Y 4LE
(Charity Registration No. 208 223)

Distributed worldwide by the Brookings Institution,
1775 Massachusetts Avenue, NW, Washington, DC 20036-2188

ISBN 1 86203 166 5

Cover design by Matthew Link
Typeset in ITC Giovanni by Koinonia, Manchester
Printed and bound in Great Britain by J. W. Arrowsmith Ltd

CONTENTS

PREFACE

The need for a reasoned Israeli debate on policy alternatives with respect to the Palestinians was identified in
spring 2003, when the conflict was at its most intense
and many Israelis, reeling in the face of suicide bomb
attacks, were inclined toward actions motivated by anger
more than judgment. At the time, many had the feeling
that the Israeli government lacked a master plan or
vision and that Israel, in a reactive and defensive mode,
might take decisions that could critically affect its room
for manoeuvre and subsequent range of options. That
was the context of the decision to consult a group of
Israeli policy analysts and advocates in the expectation
that their systematic deliberations would engage the
Israeli public on the consequences of alternative
approaches to the Palestinians by the Israeli political
leadership. The results of that consultation are presented in this volume, which appears just when an
informal ceasefire between Israel and the Palestinians
has created enough respite for the parties to reflect once
more on their options and prospects. The timing is
therefore propitious for publishing this set of policy
proposals.

We are indebted to the Ford Foundation for being so
forthcoming with the funds needed to undertake the
project. For their guidance and meticulous editing, we are

also grateful to Margaret May, Head of the Publications Department, and her colleagues at Chatham House. Most of all we thank the authors of the papers presented here for their commitment and engagement with the whole endeavour. We hope that publication of their work will prompt them to engage others in Israel and in the media generally on the issues at stake and the options they perceive.

March 2005   Mark Heller
                                                                Rosemary Hollis

ABOUT THE CONTRIBUTORS

Uzi Arad, formerly a policy adviser to Prime Minister Binyamin Netanyahu, is Director of the Institute for Policy and Strategy at the Interdisciplinary Centre, Herzliya.

Orit Gal is a PhD candidate in the Department of International Relations, Hebrew University of Jerusalem, and project director at the Economic Cooperation Foundation, Tel Aviv.

Israel Harel is President of the Israel Institute of Jewish Leadership and Strategy and writes a weekly column in *Ha'aretz* newspaper. A founder of Yesha, the highest body of the settler movement, he has served as its Chairman and as the editor of its journal, Nekuda.

Mark A. Heller is Director of Research at the Jaffee Centre for Strategic Studies, Tel Aviv University.

Rosemary Hollis is Director of Research at Chatham House, where she was previously Head of the Middle East Programme from 1995 to 2005.

David Kimche, formerly Director-General of the Israeli Foreign Ministry and an Ambassador-at-Large, is a member of the Hebrew University Board of Governors. A co-founder of the International Alliance for Arab-Israeli Peace, he is active in other peace organizations.

Joel Peters is Senior Lecturer in the Department of Politics and Government and Director of the Centre for the Study of European Politics and Society at Ben Gurion University of the Negev.

Dan Schueftan is a senior fellow at The National Security Studies Centre of the University of Haifa. He teaches at the School of Political Sciences of the University of Haifa and at the National Security College and the Command and Staff College of the Israel Defense Forces.

INTRODUCTION

Rosemary Hollis

Five alternative policy prescriptions for Israel, *vis-à-vis* relations with the Palestinians, are posited here. The case for each is made by an author or authors who, having weighed the alternatives, have come to the conclusion that theirs is the best way forward available to Israel in the current circumstances.

The five policy options are:
1. Negotiations for a permanent status agreement;
2. Preserve the Land;
3. Interim arrangements and conflict management;
4. International intervention for conflict management and resolution;
5. Unilateral disengagement.

In essence the five policy prescriptions can be encapsulated as follows:

(1) Negotiations for a permanent status agreement to begin at once, while implementing the so-called 'Road Map' (for details see below) – this prescription uses the 'Geneva initiative' as inspiration and guideline for defining an end to the conflict (namely a two-state solution) and argues that unilateral actions will not bring peace.

(2) Unilateral extension of Israeli sovereignty through annexation of areas of the West Bank currently

1

under direct Israeli security control – ('Area C' as defined under the Oslo process – see Map 2 in Appendix) but not Palestinian population centres or the Gaza Strip. Looks to Egypt and Jordan, not Israel, to accommodate Palestinian statehood in the future.

(3) A gradualist approach using sequential interim arrangements for conflict management until circumstances are more conducive to peacemaking. Argues that neither resort to final status negotiations now nor unilateral moves which require international mediation can work, and opts for several years of interim negotiations to contain the conflict until the parties, the situation and the atmosphere change.

(4) Introducing an international presence to facilitate negotiations for and implementation of a two-state solution. Claims that direct engagement of the international community and the presence of an international force on the ground are needed to help the parties towards conflict resolution.

(5) Unilateral disengagement – separating Israel from the Gaza Strip and Palestinian population centres beyond the 'security barrier' in the West Bank, with this arrangement enduring until Israelis feel assured that the Palestinians (not just the leadership) will cease using terror tactics against them and accept and abide by a compromise deal.

In developing their arguments, the authors have each identified and ranked in order of priority the core values and goals for the state of Israel which they are seeking to

2

defend and promote. They spell out their assumptions about the Palestinians (for example what is needed to obtain a deal and what a deal is worth); the likely behaviour and importance of other actors (the Arab states, Americans, Europeans); the resources available to Israel to pursue various options; and the level of urgency (effect of time). Whether implicitly or explicitly, each author also undertakes some cost/benefit and risk/opportunity analysis.

The development of all five policy options involved two levels of consultations. In the first instance, draft papers were discussed among the authors with input from some Palestinian, other Arab and international interlocutors. None of these were involved in the initial drafting or in any form of negotiation over or endorsement of any of the proposals. The purpose at that stage was simply to gain feedback on how each policy proposal was likely to be perceived and received at the Palestinian, regional and international levels. The second stage of consultations was between all the authors of the papers and the two co-directors of the project, Mark Heller and Rosemary Hollis.

The authors agreed that Israel's core values or goals are:

- a Jewish state
- a democratic state
- the land of Israel
- a secure state
- a state at peace with its neighbours.

All would like to achieve all these goals simultaneously, but if forced to accept a trade-off between them, they would rank them differently. Some would add the goal of 'strength' as a necessary condition for safety, and may contend that peace is not attainable now. Others say that peace is the only recipe for security. Reliance on third parties was considered unacceptable by some and a necessity for peace by others.

Comparisons and contrasts between the five options are made in the conclusion. Here only a short summary of each is offered by way of introduction to the full papers that follow. The exact meaning, parameters and implications of each policy prescription can only be understood by reading the work of each policy option proponent in full.

The views expressed in each individual contribution are those of the authors alone. Their inclusion here should not be taken as endorsement by either the editors or the publisher (Chatham House). Both severally and collectively they may surprise some and alienate others. Yet the purpose of the exercise is to reflect the range of opinions among Israelis and stimulate awareness and debate about policy alternatives and their implications.

1. Negotiations for a permanent status agreement, by David Kimche

Kimche's view is that Israel's goals should be the same as those of the pioneers of Zionism, namely: 'a Jewish, democratic state living at peace with its neighbours, enabling its citizens to live normal lives in accordance with accepted norms and values of an enlightened democratic society'. The only way to achieve these in current circumstances, he contends, is 'by negotiations with the Palestinians for a permanent settlement that will establish a viable Palestinian State in that part of the ancient Land of Israel defined around the world as "occupied territories"'.

His operating assumption is that there *is* a Palestinian partner with whom to negotiate peace. The 'Geneva Accord' (see Chapter 1 for details) may not be exactly the right blueprint, but it demonstrates that this is possible. The Palestinian Authority (PA), with backing from Egypt and the Arab League, is eager to negotiate, but conditions set by Israel for negotiations to resume have been beyond the practical ability of the PA to fulfil without Israeli assistance. Had Israel undertaken confidence-building measures proposed in the Quartet 'Road Map' and apparently accepted by Israel when Mahmoud Abbas (also known as Abu Mazen) was Palestinian Prime Minister, he could have moved forward on his side. The election of Abbas as President of the PA (and Chairman of the Palestine Liberation Organization) is an opportunity to remedy that earlier mistake.

Kimche's prescription is that the Israelis and Palestinians work in tandem to implement the confidence-building measures outlined in the Road Map, while the Arab states and international community, principally the United States, bolster the process. The Palestinians must take practical steps to dismantle Palestinian paramilitary organizations and implement real reforms of the PA. They have the capability to take these measures, he believes, provided the overall climate is changed.

Israel can create this change with the following confidence-building measures: removal of illegal settlement outposts; removal of roadblocks impeding movement of Palestinians between their population centres; release of more Palestinian 'security prisoners' held by Israel; provision of more permits for Palestinians to work in Israel; and redeployment of Israeli forces out of the areas occupied since the beginning of the *intifada* in September 2000.

The international community has to be an active facilitator, and should set up an international monitoring group to oversee implementation of the Road Map. Kimche says that the understandings reached between the unofficial, but nonetheless serious, negotiators of the Geneva Accord provide guidelines for implementation of the third phase of the Road Map – official negotiations – and the parties will find it easier to implement the earlier phases if they have a clear picture of what the final outcome of negotiations can be.

Unilateral separation can only work if it roughly follows the 1967 'Green Line' (see Map 3). If it falls short of this and is done piecemeal, Kimche believes it will only provide an incentive for further Palestinian violence to gain more territory. He asserts that the policy of Prime Minister Sharon is to create a long-term interim arrangement, during which Israel will tighten its hold on those parts of the West Bank that it wishes to integrate into Israel. If this negates the possibility of a viable independent Palestinian state, Kimche concludes, then demands for 'a binational state in which the Jewish people will be a minority' will become irresistible.

2. Preserve the Land, by Israel Harel

As noted by Mark Heller in Chapter 6, Harel's proposals represent the 'status quo' option, designed to protect Israel's territorial reach.

For Israel Harel, the Land of Israel (*Eretz Israel*) is essential to the identity and heritage of the Jews and is 'the only legitimate territorial basis for the realization of the Jewish people's political sovereignty'. The state must continue to be a democracy, with a Jewish majority and Jewish identity enshrined in a constitution. Security through strength is a necessity. Peace is desirable, but if to attain it 'Israel must give up large sections of its historical territorial homeland or concede its Jewish identity', then 'a state without peace is preferable'.

The religious and historical bond between the Jewish people and the Land of Israel has been accorded international recognition, says Harel, notably in the League of Nations endorsement of the Balfour Declaration (in the Mandate for Palestine given to Britain in 1922 – see Map 1). Yet, Harel laments, the British carved up the region such that Israel has been expected to make do with a small corner of the region, while the Arab nation ended up with more than 20 separate states. Even so, Israel has been willing to make compromises, but on the whole the Arabs have not. Israel agreed to the UN Partition Plan (for Mandate Palestine) of 1947; the Arabs did not and fought to try to prevent the state of Israel existing at all. Successive wars and continuing terrorism convince Harel that the Arabs still do not accept Israel. And he thinks that Israel's concessions of land for peace, as with the vast majority of territory it captured in the

1967 war, send the message that more pressure will bring more Israeli retreats. He wants to call a stop to this process of attrition, as he sees it.

Harel's central operating assumption is that while the Palestinians 'purport to want a state alongside Israel, this is not really the case'. Instead, he contends, they really want Israel not to exist, though he suspects that their reasons for this are as much practical as ideological. He thinks the Palestinians must have worked out what he believes, namely that not even the entirety of the West Bank and Gaza would make a viable Palestinian state. The reason, he says, is demography – Gaza is already an overcrowded slum. So, while he agrees with Ariel Sharon that unilateral measures are Israel's only recourse now, Harel's goal is different.

He proposes that Israel divest itself of the Gaza Strip and Palestinian population centres in the West Bank (Areas A and B under the Oslo process), wherein the Palestinians already have self-rule which he deems tantamount to sovereignty. The remainder (Area C) should be annexed to Israel. Since only a small proportion of West Bank Palestinians live in the villages in this area, Harel argues, giving them citizenship need not undermine Israel's Jewish majority, provided there is more Jewish immigration and Palestinian citizens of Israel agree to pledge allegiance to a constitution that enshrines the Jewish identity of the state.

The prescription for a regional settlement proposed by Harel requires Egypt and Jordan to shoulder the burden of making Palestinian statehood possible. Egypt could make Gaza liveable, he contends, by donating to it the northern portion of the Sinai Peninsula, for the Palestinians to populate and develop. He proposes that West Bank Palestinian population centres be attached to Jordan by east–west corridors. He takes it as read that demographic trends will eventually turn Jordan into a Palestinian state and that the non-Palestinian population can be persuaded to accept the inevitable.

Harel rests his case that Egypt and Jordan will reach an accommodation with his proposals on two arguments. First, their governments want to help the Palestinians and would benefit from an end to the Israeli–Palestinian conflict. Secondly, over time ideas have changed about how to divide the region into states, and a further change can eventually gain credibility.

3. Interim arrangements and conflict management, by Uzi Arad

Uzi Arad starts from the premise that neither direct negotiations nor unilateral Israeli moves will serve Israeli interests at this time. He therefore does not see fit to rank Israel's core values or goals in order of priority, because there is, as yet, no trade-off to be made. He concentrates instead on designing a way to manage the conflict until circumstances change and final status negotiations can be contemplated.

Arad argues that the 'Geneva Initiative' is misguided in principle and unacceptable in specifics. He refutes the contention (made here by Kimche) that the initiative demonstrates there is a Palestinian partner for peace, on the grounds that the parties to that initiative do not speak for their respective leaderships or communities.

Unless and until the Palestinians reform their whole political, financial and security system they can neither run a state nor deliver peace. On the specifics of the Geneva Accord, Arad deems the provisions for resolution of the refugee issue to be positively dangerous and not sufficient to 'end all claims'.

With respect to Ariel Sharon's so-called 'unilateral disengagement initiative', Arad argues that it is not unilateral at all. It involves Israeli negotiations with the Americans and also the Europeans. The latter, if not the former, are intent on involving the Palestinians in their deliberations about their role following disengagement. Egypt and Jordan are also to be involved in realization of the disengagement. Consequently, far from being a unilateralist initiative, it actually means an expansion of the number of parties involved. The formula compounds rather than resolves the problems facing direct negotiations.

Arad's policy prescription is a new step-by-step, open-ended process, building on the Oslo precedent and incorporating the Road Map. This would have two facets – one to move incrementally toward negotiations over the big issues; the other to change the chemistry of relations.

The first step would be a preliminary phase to precede implementation of the first phase of the Road Map. Additional phases would be inserted along the way, before final status negotiations can be launched. The Palestinians would focus on reform and possibly achieving a truce among the factions, while the Israelis would take steps to remove isolated settlement outposts and road blocks in order to facilitate Palestinian economic activity. At the same time, Israel would finish building the 'security barrier' in the West Bank, potentially subject to removal in a final status agreement.

Meanwhile, Arad hopes, a transformation could be effected in the nature of the parties and thence the nature of the conflict. Using the analogy of the slow, open-ended process by which the European Economic Community evolved over decades into the European Union, he foresees something new and as yet unpredictable emerging in the Israeli–Palestinian relationship. He anticipates this will not emerge for a decade or more.

4. International intervention for conflict management and resolution, by Joel Peters and Orit Gal

Joel Peters and Orit Gal depict a formula for peace that will protect Israel's democracy, Jewish identity and security. The price will be land, the West Bank and Gaza, which they believe must be relinquished to enable the establishment of a Palestinian state living in peace alongside Israel. The rewards will include international approval, economic investment and good-neighbourly relations. The key ingredient to make this possible, they believe, is an international presence to oversee and support implementation of the vision, but not to impose itself against the will of the parties or act as a trustee for Palestinian statehood.

The underlying assumptions here have to do with the loss of trust between the parties as a result of the collapse of the Oslo process and renewed conflict. Israelis came to believe that they have no Palestinian partner for peace and that the PA cannot deliver. Both parties accepted the Road Map but actually did not believe in it, Peters and Gal assert, and therefore they used it to gain room for manoeuvre or take advantage. They also contend that the Israeli government's subsequent adoption of a unilateralist approach is about conflict management, and that it lacks a strategic vision.

International intervention is presented as the prescription for addressing the short-termism and distrust that have prevented conflict resolution. An international peacekeeping mission, with military and civilian components, 'would be entrusted with stabilizing the situation on the ground, assisting the Palestinians with rebuilding their governance and security capacities, serving as a catalyst for reviving the peace process, and addressing the broader conflict environment'. In effect, this would mean Israel 'bestowing on the international community a stake and responsibility for the emergence of a Palestinian political entity committed to peaceful coexistence'.

Peters and Gal do not see international intervention as substituting for a peace process. They want this process revived and objectives and timetables agreed from the outset. Otherwise, a foreign presence cannot expect to receive either cooperation and acceptance on the ground or international legitimacy. Deployment of the foreign force would accompany Israeli withdrawal from Gaza and Palestinian population centres in the West Bank. The force would be charged with holding the

Palestinians to their undertakings to prevent terrorism. But it will not substitute for the PA.

A US-led force, with components from Europe (NATO) and maybe Australia and Canada, is envisaged. Its functions will include: supervision; capacity-building and coordination; monitoring and legitimacy building. Peters and Gal want this force to have the authority to mediate and guide the whole process through to implementation of a peace treaty. Incentives to the parties will include new or enhanced arrangements with the EU and NATO, and other bodies and networks.

5. Unilateral disengagement, by Dan Schueftan

Dan Schueftan considers peace desirable but unattainable and dangerous to pursue in the current circumstances. His overriding goal is a Jewish, democratic and secure Israel. He calculates that achieving and safeguarding this central objective necessitates Israeli disengagement from Palestinian population centres in the West Bank and Gaza Strip.

It is Schueftan's conviction that the Israeli people generally, though not necessarily their politicians, have come to the conclusion that a negotiated land-for-peace compromise deal is not feasible. Nor is maintaining Israeli strategic control of the West Bank and Gaza while offering the Palestinians self-government a viable solution. Schueftan also claims that it is not only the Palestinian leadership, but also the general Palestinian population, who do not represent a partner for peace. In this assessment, Schueftan believes he speaks for the general public in Israel, or a body of opinion which he calls 'mainstream Jews'. He suspects that even if his prescription is not everyone's first preference, it is most people's default option if the ideal of peace and trust is lacking.

Schueftan advocates immediate completion of the security barrier in the West Bank, along a route which ensures that the maximum number of Jewish settlers are on the Israeli side and the main Palestinian population centres are on the other side. He then envisages a withdrawal from settlements east of the barrier and in the Gaza Strip. In the end he wants total separation between the two populations and the territory in which they currently live. 'Palestinians wishing to cross the barrier into Israel will have to produce documentation and undergo a security check similar to those required when crossing other international gateways.' Israel will retain three major settlement blocks, East Jerusalem and a strip along the river Jordan and the Dead Sea. 'Most of the Jewish *settlers*, about three-quarters of them, will stay under Israeli control; most of the *settlements* and outposts, more than one hundred, will be dismantled or relocated either behind the pre-1967 lines (primarily in Galilee and the Negev) or to the retained settlement blocks.'

It is anticipated that the Palestinians will have autonomous control within the Gaza Strip and over a contiguous area in the West Bank, with north–south links around Jerusalem criss-crossing Israeli east–west links, in a series of tunnels and bridges. Pending a final peace agreement, 'Israel will maintain strict security controls

14

over the external borders of the Palestinian territories'. If they wish, the Palestinians can unilaterally declare a state, although Israel will not recognize it as sovereign until a peace deal is finally in place.

Before that can come about, the Israelis will need to be satisfied that the Palestinians are truly ready to compromise. Then Schueftan envisages discussing permanent international borders, though Israel's position on the route these should take and the extent of the limitations on Palestinian sovereignty will depend on what has happened in the intervening period. Israelis will want to be convinced that the Palestinians are no longer committed to a strategy of terror. The final status agreement will also depend, he says, 'on unequivocal Palestinian public acceptance of the legitimacy of a *Jewish* nation-state within the borders that will be agreed upon, alongside the Palestinian *Arab* nation-state'.

Pending Palestinian acceptance of negotiations on these terms, Schueftan proposes that Israel continue to manage the situation through unilateral decisions and actions. He looks to the international community for little. US support is valued and acknowledged, but in Schueftan's view the Europeans are so prejudiced against the Israelis that they can be expected to be critical of whatever Israel does, and so European opinion should not be a consideration.

Implications

Each of the policy options presented here speaks for a section of Israeli public opinion. Together they reveal the absence of a consensus not only on policy prescriptions but also on objectives. A reading of the five proposals also shows how dependent each is on the author's assumptions about the other parties to the Arab–Israeli conflict and in the international community. All are clear about what it is they are trying to protect, preserve and build, but the prescriptions they offer are based on a combination of preferences and assessments of 'the other' which tend to reinforce their arguments.

By implication, as discussed in the conclusion at the end of this volume, what is needed now is a parallel study on Palestinian perspectives and policy options, as a prelude to a more comprehensive analysis of alternative ways forward. For now, however, the purpose is to generate greater awareness, not only of the policy options, but also of the choices already being made, rejected or ignored.

1 NEGOTIATIONS FOR A PERMANENT STATUS AGREEMENT

David Kimche

Goals and values

The pioneers who over the years re-established a strong Jewish presence in the Land of Israel were motivated by the Zionist ideal of the return of the Jews to their ancient homeland. Their aim was to create a Jewish state in which its inhabitants could live normal lives in peace and security, in contrast to the way of life of the Jews of the Diaspora, in particular of those Jews living in abject conditions in eastern Europe. The Zionist leaders in time defined their aims more clearly: the Jewish state must be democratic and must be driven by a high standard of morals and values – in the words of the Zionist philosopher Ahad Ha'am, the Jewish state should be *'A Light unto the Nations'*.

The driving force of Israel today should be those same goals: a Jewish, democratic state living at peace with its neighbours and enabling its citizens to live normal lives in accordance with the accepted norms and values of an enlightened democratic society. The only way in which Israel can achieve these aims in its present situation is by negotiations with the Palestinians for a permanent settlement that will establish a viable Palestinian state in that part of the ancient Land of Israel defined around the world as 'occupied territories'.

As long as Israel continues to rule the Palestinians

living in those territories, its morals and values will be circumscribed, its democratic foundations will be threatened and its Jewish character will be undermined. It is already an accepted fact that within a few years, the Jewish population in the territory between the river Jordan and the Mediterranean will be in the minority. It is argued that this will not affect the democratic character of the State of Israel, as there is no intention to annex the 'territories'. More recently, it has been argued that if Israel leaves the Gaza Strip, the demographic equation will change to its advantage.

Although there may be some truth in these arguments, the fact remains that continued rule over another people creates an apartheid-type situation that cannot but affect both the value system of the Israeli society and its democratic character. Moreover, with the continued Jewish presence in the heartland of Judea and Samaria, there can be no possibility of establishing a viable Palestinian state. Even if Israel has no intention to annex these territories, the present status quo, that is the conflict between 'occupiers' and 'occupied', cannot continue indefinitely. If an independent Palestinian state is indeed ruled out because of the Israeli presence in Judea and Samaria, then outside pressure and Palestinian demands will eventually bring about the alternative – a binational state in which the Jewish people will be a minority. The alternatives then facing the Jewish population of Israel would be to continue ruling by relinquishing the democratic character of the state or to maintain democracy but then to surrender Jewish rule over the state. Israel would become either less Jewish or less democratic. In either case, the Zionist ideal would be forfeited.

Operating assumptions

Following the resumption of conflict in late 2000, innumerable newspaper articles, media programmes and speeches demonstrated that both Israelis and Palestinians thought they had no partner for peace 'on the other side'. The prevalence of this assumption has led to the dismissal of a negotiated settlement as a viable possibility. Instead, Israel has proposed a unilateral initiative to withdraw from Gaza and parts of the northern West Bank. But even before the demise of Yasser Arafat, the assumption that there is no partner for peace had been disproved – by the unofficial Geneva Accord (discussed in more detail below) and by the endorsement by large numbers of Palestinians and Israelis of the Ayalon-Nusseibeh document.[1] There can be no doubt that the conditions set forth by the Sharon government for meaningful peace negotiations have largely negated any possibility of talks taking place. By making the negotiations conditional on an end to terrorism, the government was in effect saying to all those Palestinians who opposed making peace with Israel: 'All you have to do to prevent peace negotiations is to continue terror attacks!'

During the first phase of the *intifada* beginning in 2000, the government's demand was for a period of absolute quiet as a precondition for negotiations. It was enough for the army to report that shots were fired to establish that this condition had not been met. A number

[1] In July 2002, Professor Sari Nusseibeh of Palestine and the former head of the Israeli Security Service, Ami Ayalon, signed a Statement of Principles outlining the main elements of a future peace agreement. Since then, tens of thousands of Israelis and Palestinians have signed petitions supporting the Statement.

of cease-fire arrangements were put in place, but neither the Palestinians nor the Israeli army respected them.

At a later stage of the *intifada*, the demand for a period of quiet was abandoned (at the insistence of the Americans) and replaced by the condition that the Palestinian Authority dismantle the terrorist groups before negotiations begin. This condition was accepted as valid by the United States and by the international community. It forms one of the demands of the Road Map, the prescription for moving towards peace formulated by the Quartet of the United States, the European Union, Russia and the United Nations.

There can be no doubt that this stipulation was a valid one, logical and justified. But how realistic has it been? The Palestinian Authority, severely weakened by the *intifada*, was hardly in a position to embark on what could become virtually a civil war against Hamas and Islamic Jihad. Its security forces were crippled by repeated Israeli strikes against them and it needed time and outside help in order to reconstruct them and to strengthen its authority. In particular, it needed, at the very least, the support of the Palestinian population, and it could obtain such support only if it could show that it was gaining advantages for the people in return for turning against the terrorist groups. This, in turn, could be achieved only by Israeli confidence-building measures in the form of the release of prisoners, the removal of roadblocks, the ending of closures of Palestinian towns and villages, etc. This was the deal that Mahmoud Abbas (Abu Mazen) sought to obtain when he became Palestinian prime minister in 2003. Then, unfortunately, the

Israeli government was not accommodating, and the vicious cycle of violence and counter-violence continued.

On the Palestinian side, there was no desire to deal with the terrorist groups without first receiving concessions from Israel. But Israel was unwilling to make any concessions without the Palestinians first tackling the terrorists. Without such concessions or confidence-building measures, the Palestinians would not go to war against Hamas. Without such a move to curb terrorism, Israel would not make concessions or undertake negotiations for a permanent settlement. Thus, the assumptions that there were no partners for peace and that the stalemate could therefore be broken only by unilateral measures gained credence.

Yet it could have been otherwise and may yet be. Even before Mahmoud Abbas succeeded Yasser Arafat, the Palestinian Authority was eager to enter into negotiations. Moreover, it was encouraged to do so by the Egyptians and, indeed, by the entire Arab world. The Arab League initiative adopted at the summit of Arab heads of state in Beirut in 2002, which called for peace with all Arab countries in return for a withdrawal by Israel to the 1967 'Green Line', was the clearest indication yet that the Arab countries are sick and tired of the Palestinian–Israeli conflict and want nothing more than to see the end of it.

This attitude largely reflects the feelings prevalent in other parts of the world, particularly in Europe, where Israel is increasingly held responsible for the lack of any movement towards a negotiated permanent settlement. Growing anti-Israeli sentiments, often translated into open anti-Semitic acts, indicate that Israel is losing the battle for world public opinion, at least in Europe. The comparison of Israel to South Africa in the apartheid period is gathering momentum, and it is fuelled by the negative public relations impact of the security barrier. Although the United States has been much more understanding of Israel's position than have the European countries, continued support for Israel from that crucial quarter is not necessarily a foregone conclusion. The American imbroglio in Iraq, the hostility of the Muslim world to the United States, the need in the post-election period to coordinate more with Europe, and the determination of President Bush in his second term of office to realize his vision of a two-state solution – Israel and an independent Palestine side by side – are all factors influencing US policy.

Thus time is not necessarily playing in favour of Israel, as the Israeli government has assumed. On the contrary, a continued deterioration in Israel's standing in the world could be fraught with danger, and should be an added incentive for the Israeli government to address itself urgently to ending the stalemate. However, unilateral actions – even if they entail withdrawing from the Gaza Strip – will not in themselves provide the answer.

The policy prescription

Israel has, rightly, repeatedly declared that it considers the Road Map to be the only existing official policy proposal that can point the way to an end to the conflict. Time and again it has declared, correctly, that for the Road Map to be implemented, the Palestinians need to take practical steps to dismantle the terror groups, which, as of this writing, they have refused to do for the reasons stated above. As a result, there has been stalemate. It must be stressed that the status quo of early 2005 is not sustainable; and if there is no move forward, there will be further deterioration. Terror and counter-strikes will continue, and will not be eliminated by just a unilateral Israeli withdrawal from the Gaza Strip.

The imperative, therefore, is to create a plan for implementing the Road Map that must include actions, such as those outlined below, not as an end in them-selves but as a prelude to peace negotiations. Not only the Palestinians and the Israelis, but also the Arab world and the international community, especially the United States, will have to be involved.

The Palestinians

The Palestinian Authority must accept the basic fact that as long as independent militias exist, there can be no real progress towards peace, nor can any Palestinian government exercise authority fully over its own people. It must take practical steps to dismantle these indepen-dent military groups. It must make clear that it will not tolerate illegal weapons or ammunition stockpiles, that workshops for the production of weapons will be des-troyed and that strong measures will be taken against those who flout the directives of the Palestinian Authority. Moreover, the Palestinians must make every effort to complete the reforms as stipulated in the Road Map. Yasser Arafat had been the major obstacle to those reforms. His death has made it much easier to implement them because his successors and, indeed, much of Palestinian society, had wanted to introduce reforms, and it was only the stand taken by Arafat against any changes that had prevented them from doing so.

Can the Palestinian Authority fulfil all these conditions? It can, if it gets help from Israel and the international community. Palestinian security officers estimate that they could bring a semblance of order to the West Bank within a month if they received such help. It would take them longer in the Gaza Strip, not only because of the strength of Hamas but also because of the internal jockeying for power among the Fatah personnel there and the lack of a unified stand against Hamas. They are, however, confident they could deal with the present security problems provided the overall climate changes. This means, first and foremost, a willingness on the part of Israel to help them.

The Israelis

Israel must understand that for the Palestinians to take the steps described above, it must be serious about the promised confidence-building measures, discussed between Sharon and Abbas after their Sharm el Sheik summit in February 2005.

(a) *Removal of illegal settlement outposts.* These outposts constitute a flagrant violation of Israeli law, with all that such a breach implies. Their continued existence contravenes the Road Map and the promise made by the prime minister to the president of the United States. As long as they remain in place, Israel's word cannot be taken seriously.

(b) *Removal of roadblocks.* Dozens of roadblocks have been created since 2000, not only on roads leading to Israel but mainly between Palestinian towns and villages. Villages have been almost totally cut off from their provincial centres, causing untold hardship and massive unemployment, and undermining any semblance of normal life. A gradual restoration of freedom of movement between towns and villages for the Palestinians is an essential prerequisite for progress towards implementation of the Road Map.

(c) *Release of prisoners.* Of the more than 6,000 security prisoners held by Israel in recent years, only some 600 could be defined as having 'blood on their hands'. Israel could therefore release a significantly larger number than the 550 offered during the negotiations with then Prime Minister Abu Mazen in 2003 and again at the beginning of his presidency.

(d) *Increased number of work permits.* Their number should be increased significantly in order to alleviate the current lack of employment. This is only one of the steps that would be needed to help change the dire social conditions existing among the Palestinians. An economic Road Map would have to be put in place, with the help of Europe and the United States, once the provisions of the existing Road Map were met.

(e) *Redeployments.* There should be a clear undertaking to withdraw from the areas occupied since the beginning of the *intifada* once the Palestinians fulfil their own promises with regard to dismantling the terrorist groups.

To implement all these gestures will not be easy – probably it will be as difficult for the Israeli government to take such steps as it will be for the Palestinian Authority to deal with Hamas. The internal political scene would be thrown into complete disarray. Yet without such moves by both the Israelis and the Palestinians, there will be no implementation of the Road Map, no move to direct negotiations and no possibility of a peaceful solution to the conflict.

The international community

All these efforts will be useless without the active involvement of the international community, including but not limited to an effective international monitoring group that would oversee the implementation of the phases of the Road Map. The appointment of Lt. Gen. William Ward in early February 2005 as a monitor of security cooperation is a start, but more effort will be required to see through implementation of the Road Map.

Above all, the United States and the other members of the Quartet should actively press upon Israel and the Palestinian Authority the need to take all the steps outlined above in order to enter into negotiations for a permanent settlement of the conflict as soon as possible. Both sides to the conflict should be given to understand that they have much to gain by moving towards implementing the Road Map and entering into negotiations and, equally, that they have much to lose if they do not follow that route.

Can it be done? Those who believe in an interim agreement, in maintaining the status quo, or in a unilateral withdrawal, have argued that negotiations for a permanent status agreement are not feasible because there are no partners for peace. 'There is no one to talk to and nothing to talk about' or 'the Palestinians will never make peace with us' are phrases heard often in recent times. Such convictions gave legitimacy to the Israeli government's policy of military rather than political options and, more recently, of unilateral withdrawal. However the validity of these arguments has been undermined by the Geneva Accord, a comprehensive model agreement that was reached in a Jordanian hotel at the Dead Sea on 12 October 2003. The 44-page document, along with the map that defines the borders of the two states, belie the statement that there are no partners for peace.

The Geneva Accord

In contrast to the Oslo Agreements and the Road Map, the Geneva Accord deals with the most critical and sensitive of the issues that have divided Israelis and Palestinians. Instead of the gradualist approach that characterized the Oslo Agreements – of moving step by step in order to build up trust and leaving the difficult problems to the end – the Geneva understandings tackled all the problems that have bedevilled relations between the two peoples. Instead of leaving the end results vague, as in the Road Map, the negotiators at the Dead Sea meeting drew a comprehensive picture of the final outcome of the negotiations. In no way did these understandings contradict the Road Map or claim to replace that policy proposal. On the contrary, the Geneva signatories viewed their document as fleshing out the third phase of the Road Map.

The Palestinian delegation included three former ministers as well as leaders of the Tanzim, the militant 'Young Turks' of the Fatah Movement. After agreement was finally reached at the concluding plenary, the head of the Palestinian team, Yasser abed Rabbo, announced that Yasser Arafat, Ahmad Qurei (Abu Ala) and Mahmoud Abbas all voiced their support. It thus became clear that this was a serious effort on the part of the Palestinians to reach an agreement with the Israelis. It was not a fly-by-night affair but rather an acceptance of the Geneva Accord by their highest authorities. Some of the most active among the Palestinian negotiators were appointed ministers in the Palestinian government that was formed after the Geneva Accord was signed. One of the closest associates of Yasser Arafat was sent to Geneva to be present at the ceremony that was held to mark the signing of the accord. Osama el-Baz, adviser to Egypt's President Mubarak, was also conspicuous among those attending the Geneva ceremony.

Of course, future negotiations between the Israeli government and the Palestinian Authority do not have to incorporate all the clauses of the 44-page Geneva document, which was not negotiated by official government representatives. The agreement reached by the Israelis and the Palestinians was virtual and non-binding. Its main objective was educational – to demonstrate to both the Israeli public and the Palestinian public that an agreement is possible and that there are indeed partners for peace on 'the other side'. The final negotiations may differ in many ways from the Geneva Accord but the two years of negotiations which preceded its signing did reveal what could and could not be accepted by both sides. For that reason, the Geneva Accord provides revealing guidelines regarding future official negotiations.

Thus it became clear to the Palestinian negotiators that their insistence on including the Right of Return of Palestinian refugees was a deal-breaker for the Israelis, who would have terminated the talks if the Palestinians had persisted in demanding its inclusion. Similarly, the Israelis discovered that the Palestinians would have left the negotiation table if they were not granted sovereignty over the Temple Mount. These were red lines that the two sides were not prepared to cross, even if that meant the failure of the talks. Conversely, the Palestinians were willing to agree to Israeli demands that the Palestinian state recognize Israel as the home of the Jewish people and that the agreement would mark the end of the conflict between the two peoples. The Israelis, for their part, accepted the principle of withdrawal to the 1967 demarcation lines, with concomitant equal compensation of land for the territory that would remain under Israeli jurisdiction. Both sides accepted the division of Jerusalem according to the principle laid down by President Clinton that Palestinian-populated areas would be part of the Palestinian capital and those areas inhabited by Jews would be part of the capital of Israel.

Any future official negotiations will have to be based

on these fundamental principles. It is hard to imagine either side compromising on any of them. However, the details may well be changed. For example, Israel may insist that the settlement of Ariel be included in the territory it wishes to keep in exchange for a slice of land it will give in return. It may well demand more forthright language describing Palestinian recognition of Israel as a Jewish state. The Palestinians may have similar demands.

Other aspects of the Geneva Accord that will doubtless form the basis for future negotiations include the following:

- All aspects of violence and terrorism against each other and in general will be eradicated and a special trilateral security committee will be established to ensure full implementation.

- The Palestinians will agree to two Israeli early warning stations on their territory, as well as an Israel Defense Forces (IDF) presence in the Jordan Valley, for an agreed period of time.

- The Israeli air force will be entitled to use Palestinian airspace for training purposes.

- The Palestinian state will be demilitarized.

- An implementation and verification group will be established, as well as a multinational force, in order to ensure full implementation of the agreement, to provide security to the demilitarized state of Palestine and to supervise border crossings.

- The agreement ends the period of conflict and settles all claims by the parties arising from events occurring prior to its signature.

- No further claims may be raised by either party.

A year before the Geneva Accord was signed, it would have been highly doubtful whether an Israeli majority would have supported such a document with its painful concessions, Palestinian sovereignty over the Temple Mount and most of the Old City, abandonment of so many settlements, an international force to supervise border crossings to Egypt and Jordan (with, however, an Israeli presence), the IDF in the Jordan Valley for only a limited time – all these concessions would have been totally unacceptable to a large segment of the population. Similarly, for most Palestinians, abandonment of the Right of Return, recognition of Israel as a Jewish state, acceptance of the end of the conflict and the continued existence of the settlement Givat Ze'ev almost on the outskirts of the Palestinian town of Ramallah and of Ma'ale Adumim east of Jerusalem would probably have been anathema. And there can be no doubt that very many Israelis and Palestinians will find it impossible to accept these conditions in the future.

However, in the fourth year of the *intifada*, realization dawned on both populations that there is no alternative to a political settlement with painful concessions by both sides. Neither the Israelis nor the Palestinians could see any hope in their present policies. Despair had become a dominant mood in both societies. Many Israelis came to understand that there could be no military solution and that maintaining the status quo would be impossible without continued violence, that the chances of large-scale international intervention were negligible and that unilateral withdrawal would not stop the violence unless it entailed going back to the 1967 lines. The Palestinians, for their part, have realized that violence and terror cannot overcome Israel and, if anything, will only harden its resolve not to make concessions. Moreover, both societies know that the tremendous economic crisis with its concomitant social malaise cannot be rectified without a peaceful solution to the conflict. It will only worsen as the weeks and months go by and violence continues. For these reasons, both societies have became more inclined to accept the conditions as put forward in the Geneva Accord, painful as they may be.

Weighing the alternatives

The cost of negotiations for both societies will be high. Yet an examination of other options reveals that their costs would be considerably higher. The principal alternative is the proposal of Prime Minister Sharon for unilateral separation. It deserves closer inspection.

Unilateral separation could be a solution, provided that the separation would be roughly along the 1967 lines. Anything less than that would be counterproductive, as it would not prevent the continuation of the violence. The Israeli–Palestinian conflict would not come to an end. On the contrary, the Palestinians would have an added incentive to increase their attacks, on the presumption that violence had led Israel to withdraw and therefore that increased violence would induce further withdrawals. The inevitable comparison with the IDF's retreat from southern Lebanon in response to

Hizbollah attacks would be made.

A withdrawal to the 1967 lines, however, need not be undertaken unilaterally. It would be far more effective if it came as a result of an agreement that heralded the end of the conflict and that would be achieved as a result of permanent status negotiations.

Nonetheless there is no intention to withdraw to anywhere near the 1967 lines, except in the Gaza Strip. The policy of the Israeli prime minister is to create a long-term interim arrangement during which no political solutions to the conflict would be sought and no negotiations for a solution would be held. The withdrawal from Gaza and from a number of isolated settlements in Judea and Samaria would, in his opinion, make it easier to attain support for the concept from the United States. It is difficult not to give backing to a plan that calls for the dismantling of the settlements in the Gaza Strip; even the Secretary-General of the Arab League, Amr Moussa, cautiously welcomed the proposed move as early as 24 February 2004.[2] Indeed, the fact that Prime Minister Sharon has called for the dismantlement of the settlements is, in itself, a major shift in the policy of the government. Israelis have called his plan 'earth-shaking'. It has certainly shaken up the internal Israeli political structure, with ramifications that have caused the reshaping of political parties and a change in the governing coalition.

According to the prime minister's concept, during the open-ended interim period Israel would tighten its hold on those parts of Judea and Samaria that it wishes to

[2] Interview with Israeli Television, 24 February 2004.

33

become part of Israel and, at the same time, evacuate many of the small, isolated settlements.

Although the decision to withdraw from the Gaza Strip has been widely welcomed, the results of such a move could be negative for the peace process if taken unilaterally without any coordination or agreement with the Palestinian Authority. The big victors in such a move could be Hamas. Moreover, as originally conceived, the message of unilateral separation is that there are no partners for peace, no possibility of entering into negotiations and therefore no alternative but to act unilaterally. Thus the basic message is that the conflict cannot be solved; it can only be contained. The enmity, the violence, the hatred will continue as before, the difference being that Israel will be deployed outside the Gaza cauldron with fewer settlements to guard and will be able to deal with the violence and the terror attacks in a more effective manner. It will, however, continue to be an occupying power. It will continue to face an increasingly negative, even hostile, world public opinion. It will continue to live in conflict and under the constant threat of terror attacks.

One could say that the intended withdrawal would make it easier to enter into meaningful negotiations after the withdrawal is completed. That is true, and that is the reason why many people in the 'peace camp' support the prime minister's plan. This, however, is not the intention of the government.

Thus the battle lines are drawn between a solution by means of negotiations and containment through unilateral separation. The former will be possible only if Palestinians and Israelis agree to fulfil the directives of the Road Map, as outlined above, and that will be possible only if there is a greater international involvement, in particular by the United States, for that purpose. As for the Israeli public, the continuing economic crisis, the worsening social malaise, the despair and the growing scepticism over the present policies of the government all combine with the new hope generated by the Geneva Accord to make it more demanding of a solution that can bring an end to the conflict. Let there be no misunderstanding: only negotiations for a permanent status agreement can solve the conflict and can bring peace to Israelis and Palestinians. Only they can bring about a viable, independent Palestinian state and achieve the objectives of Israel's forefathers, a normal, democratic, moral Jewish state. Sooner or later, Israelis and Palestinians will have to go down that route.

2 PRESERVE THE LAND
Israel Harel

Goals and values

(a) The Land of Israel

The Land of Israel, Eretz Israel, within its historical borders, is the only legitimate territorial basis for the realization of the Jewish people's political sovereignty. It belongs to the Jewish people by virtue of the political sovereignty that existed in it for hundreds of years and by virtue of 2,000 years of the Jewish people's continuous and uninterrupted longing for it. During that time, the Jewish people preserved the continuity of its manifest and unbroken bond to the Land of Israel until it decided, by means of its national movement, the Zionist movement, to return and realize in it the Jewish people's historical and national sovereignty, despite the numerous sacrifices involved.

This religious and historical bond to the land was acknowledged in the Balfour Declaration of 1917, which was in turn endorsed and adopted by the League of Nations. Britain, as mandatory power, was charged by the League with implementing Balfour's call for the establishment of a Jewish national home, and thence no doubt a state, in the land the Jews know as Eretz Israel – the approximate historical expanse of which covers parts of what became Syria, and all of what is now Jordan (and certainly the area known as the West Bank) – about

140,000 square kilometres (see Map 1). Despite this recognition, in 1922, Britain – the country that issued the Balfour Declaration – subtracted all the territory located on the eastern bank of the river Jordan, an area representing three-quarters of historical Eretz Israel, from the land to be designated for the Jewish national home. It handed over this territory to Emir Abdullah for the establishment of Trans-Jordan, one of several states created by British and French imperial manipulation in the wake of the defeat of the Ottoman Empire in the First World War. In many cases, these states were created without much attention to the implications of their artificial nature. Some of the consequences of ignoring demographic realities or geographic feasibility are still evident today – as exemplified in Iraq, where divisions between the Shiites, the Sunnis and the Kurds could undermine unified statehood.

In the wake of the Second World War, the institutions of the Jewish people who had gathered in Eretz Israel were obliged to agree to yet another partition, this time of western Eretz Israel, the part that had been designated for Jewish political sovereignty. According to the United Nations' decision of November 1947, only a small proportion of historical Eretz Israel, about 12,000 square kilometres, was ultimately to be included in Israel's share of the partition. The Jews accepted the decree. The Arabs, who were invited to establish yet another Arab state in Eretz Israel in the remaining 50 per cent of the territory west of the river Jordan (including Judea and Samaria), refused to accept the UN decision and launched a war to destroy the fledgling Jewish state.

The State of Israel, with a population of only 650,000, was simultaneously attacked by five Arab states, but it prevailed. Only three years after the terrible Holocaust in Europe had decimated the Jewish people, Israel emerged, albeit within interim, unrecognized borders – the armistice lines of 1949, later to be known as the Green Line – in an area of 20,500 square kilometres (see Map 3).

If the Arab states had been willing to agree, most of the people living in the State of Israel before June 1967 would have gladly viewed those armistice lines as the final borders of their state. But the Arabs refused to accept the outcome of the war and prepared themselves to correct a 'historical injustice'. The opportunity came in 1967 when President Gamal Abdul Nasser of Egypt closed the Straits of Tiran and, contrary to the agreement governing the Israeli withdrawal from the Sinai Peninsula in 1957, sent his army into Sinai, placing Israel in a perilous situation.

Israel was victorious in the war that ensued, which restored to it some of its historical territory, including the Old City of Jerusalem and Judea and Samaria (ruled by Jordan from 1948 to 1967). But once again, Israel expressed its willingness, in the wake of the decision made by the unity government at the time, to compromise on virtually all the territory it had acquired in the war in return for a binding contractual peace. However, a summit of all Arab countries in Khartoum in 1968 completely rejected any offers of peace and adopted its 'Three Noes' resolution: no negotiations, no recognition of Israel and no peace with the Zionist entity. 'What was taken by force', said the operative section of the Khartoum conference resolution, 'will be restored by force.' This amounted to a declaration of perpetual war on the Jewish people in its historical homeland.

(b) A democratic Israel

In its declaration of independence of May 1948, the nascent Jewish state proclaimed that it would be a democracy and would grant equal rights to all the minorities living in it regardless of religion, gender or origin. That included the Arab minority, which refused to accept its existence.

Although the Jewish people had not developed a tradition of democracy of its own – because it had been a nation in exile for over 2,000 years – Israel soon developed into an advanced political and civil democracy with a magnificent legal system worthy of any Western country that has lived independently on its own territory for hundreds of years. The Arab citizens of Israel are entitled to full rights in this democracy even though they and their Knesset representatives display sympathy for and seemingly identify with the Arab countries, many of which want the destruction of Israel as a Jewish state. Most dangerously of all, some sympathize with the terrorist organizations, and in a few cases, this identification has extended to participation in or support for terror attacks by Palestinians against Israel's Jewish citizens. The partial discrimination against Israel's Arabs is a response to this apparent divided loyalty.

In Judea and Samaria, the problem of Israel's civic responsibility for the democratic rights of the Palestinians has been dramatically reduced, as about 96 per cent of the 3.2 million Palestinians in Judea, Samaria and Gaza live under the jurisdiction of the Palestinian Authority and have the right to vote for the Palestinian parliament and the president of the Palestinian Authority. Most Palestinians live in Areas A and B, as defined in interim measures under the Oslo peace process (see Map 2). In actual fact, only about four per cent of the Palestinians, some 150,000 people, live in Area C, which has remained under full Israeli control throughout. Because Israel has already made enough territorial concessions, this area should be annexed to Israel and the Palestinians living within it should be given Israeli citizenship – if they desire it and after they have fulfilled the commonly accepted requirements regarding the granting of citizenship (study of the language, declaration of allegiance, etc.).

(c) A Jewish Israel

The Jews returned to their historical homeland in order to establish a Jewish state – not a binational state or 'a state of all its citizens' (duplicitous euphemisms used by those who aspire to destroy the Jewish state, if not by the sword then by means of the Arabs' faster population growth). The imperative for the State of Israel, therefore, is to maintain its Jewish majority. There are a number of ways this can be accomplished: increasing Jewish immigration to Israel, including from the West; clearly establishing the Jewish character of the state in a constitution; requiring all Israel's citizens, including its Arab ones, to make a declaration of allegiance to this constitution, which would include a statement regarding the

Jewish character of the state; and conferring on those who are unable for reasons of conscience to make such a declaration the status of resident aliens – similar to the status of legal aliens in the United States – while offering reasonable compensation to those who decide to emigrate.

(d) A strong and secure Israel

The war of terror has presented Israel with challenges that are difficult to deal with, as evinced by its inability to bring the current phase to a decisive end. Great powers such as Russia, the United States and Britain have no compunction about fighting terror with the same means they would use in a conventional war (that is, attacking not only combatants but also their support system and environs). But Israel is forced, owing mainly to pressure by countries that fight terror without restraint or moral qualms, to fight with its hands tied, as if it were merely policing crime. If Israel does not free itself from this pressure, the result could be no less, and perhaps even more, critical for its security than, for example, the threat from Iran.

Just as there can be no Jewish state without a Jewish majority, there can be no Jewish existence anywhere in the long run without a strong and secure Jewish state. In certain countries, such as those in Scandinavia, the rate of Jewish assimilation is as high as 85 per cent. In the United States, where the largest concentration of Jews outside the State of Israel lives, the situation is quickly approaching that of the Scandinavian countries. In 1965, there were about 6.5 million Jews in the United States.

Just 37 years later, in 2002, there were only 5.2 million. Moreover, the affiliation of many of these 5.2 million to the Jewish people is doubtful. These facts are addressed here because the continued existence of the Jewish people is the most important component of the security – and not only the physical security – of the State of Israel.

(e) Israel at peace

Peace is, and always has been, the greatest aspiration and desire of Israel and the Jewish people. The problem is that for many Israelis, in the past few years peace has no longer been a means to an end; it has become the end itself. I maintain that one of the reasons that Israelis have not been able to attain peace is that the Arabs have identified this longing as the Israelis' principal goal, but also as Israel's principal weakness, and consequently they exploit it. Seemingly, the Arabs are convinced – and it would make sense from their point of view – that if peace is the supreme goal, then there is virtually no limit to what the Jews will be willing to pay for it. They could be willing to relinquish, for example, a large amount of their homeland, and the Arabs seem to believe that each refusal to make peace will lead to an even more far-reaching Israeli offer culminating, perhaps, in the ultimate concession of Israeli independence after the Jews have been completely worn down.

Peace is a means, not an end. The goal is the existence of a Jewish state in Eretz Israel. Naturally, peace is an ideal state for the optimum development of the country. But if Israel must give up large sections of its historical territorial homeland or concede its Jewish identity, then a state without peace is preferable to one that endangers its security, Jewish identity or Jewish majority.

Operating assumptions

My working assumption is that although the Palestinians purport to want a state alongside Israel, this is not the case. What they actually want is for Israel not to exist, if only because it would be impossible to establish a viable state on the territory planned for Palestine (in the Geneva Accord, for instance), even assuming that Israel withdraws from all of it. And they are quite right. It is impossible to establish a viable state on a territory of 5,500 square kilometres – the maximum territory the Palestinian state would have if Israel were to withdraw from all of Judea, Samaria and Gaza – even in the short to medium term, and certainly not in view of the fact that the rate of natural population growth in these areas is among the highest in the world. If Israel concedes its heartland of Judea and Samaria so that the Palestinians can establish their state there, both states will soon find themselves in a situation in which they do not have sufficient land under their feet.

Israel between the river Jordan and the Mediterranean Sea covers an area of 26,000 square kilometres. About 9.5 million people currently live in this area, with an average of about 365 people per square kilometre, already one of the highest population densities in the world. And because the rate of natural growth of the Arab population is among the highest in the world – in Gaza, it is the highest – in another generation's time the density will be intolerable, because prevailing conditions do not allow for high-rise construction and the development of modern infrastructures that can prevent ecological catastrophes. About 3.25 million people, not including Jews, live in the 5,500 square kilometres that comprise Judea, Samaria and Gaza. This is a density of 590 people per square kilometre. About 1.25 million people live in Gaza, which has an area of 367 square kilometres (the area of a medium-sized ranch in the United States, Canada or Australia). According to the World Bank, the population of Gaza doubles every 17–20 years. Consequently, about 2.5 million people will be living in Gaza in the year 2020, with a density of about 7,000 people per square kilometre. About 85 per cent of the population of Gaza is under the age of 18, and the establishment of a Palestinian state would do nothing to disarm this ticking demographic time bomb. When the density there reaches a truly intolerable level, when there is not enough to eat or anywhere to go when one is ill, neither fences nor signed agreements will do any good. Therefore, another solution must be found.

Besides, the Arabs have been genuinely and seriously offered a state alongside the Jewish state a number of times since the Balfour Declaration. The first offers came in the framework of the Royal Commissions established by Britain (for example the Peel Commission of 1937) and then of the United Nations partition plan of 1947. The Oslo agreements also make this offer, as do the partition plans advanced by Ehud Barak and Bill Clinton in the 2000–01 negotiations beginning at Camp David and ending at Taba. These plans ultimately proposed handing over 97 per cent of Judea, Samaria and Gaza, including East Jerusalem, to the Palestinians for a state, in addition to three per cent from sovereign Israel. Since then, President Bush has again endorsed a Palestinian state in (it would appear) most of Judea, Samaria and Gaza.

But instead of grabbing what was offered, the Palestinians responded each time with war. In 1948, it was the full-scale war of the Arab countries against the nascent Jewish state. After the Oslo agreements, it was the suicide bombing of buses all over Israel. The response after Camp David, Taba and thereafter the launch of the Road Map was similar. This provides ample proof of the truth of my working assumption regarding the real intentions of the Palestinians.

The only possible mitigation of this assumption after more than four years of suicide terror and other acts of unspeakable horror perpetrated on Israel is the thought that the Palestinians would prefer to obtain their goals without any further acts of slaughter. This is because these acts are not very well received in other parts of the world (although in some places, and not only the Arab countries, the suicide bombers are still applauded for their 'courage'). But as the Jews continue to hold on, the war of attrition will continue until Israel is completely worn down. And all the peace plans that Jews repeatedly come up with – each of which has usually involved greater concessions than the one before – prove that the Palestinians' goal, even if delayed, will eventually be attained.

The working assumption of many Israelis – and Sharon managed to convince the first administration of George W. Bush of this – is that as long as the Arabs have not accepted the existence of a Jewish state in the Middle East, any step that Israel takes to assure its continued existence and welfare must, owing to circumstances rather than choice, be unilateral. However, in contrast to Prime Minister Ariel Sharon's unilateral steps, my point of departure is that in order to cause the world to adopt a realistic approach, Israel must take measures in which not only Israel itself but also others – especially Egypt and Jordan – are compelled to contribute to the establishment of a viable Palestinian state. I refer to their political and economic backing of the Palestinians, and especially to their material, that is, territorial, contributions. After all, the Palestinians are their flesh and blood, they are part of the same nation and share the same religion, and it was only colonial manipulation that turned the members of a single nation into 22 separate states and – in order to justify this after the fact – 22 Arab sub-nations.

The essence of a regional settlement

The whole situation could be transformed if the various actors involved would change their thinking. Ideally, the international community, led by the United States, will convince Egypt to allocate about 30,000 square kilometres in northern Sinai to the Palestinians living in the Gaza Strip. This constitutes about one-third of the Sinai Peninsula's total of 90,000 square kilometres and about 0.025 per cent of Egypt's total territory of approximately 1.2 million square kilometres. The territory is at present almost entirely uninhabited, but it has accessible groundwater for agriculture and a temperate climate. A land transfer of this magnitude would increase the area of the Gaza Strip a hundredfold and provide some living space for the people of Gaza, who – as indicated above – now have the highest rate of natural increase in the world. Incidentally, this area alone would be larger than the entire State of Israel plus Judea and Samaria, and there the large Gaza population will be able to find enough land and food. The Palestinian state would then be able to move on to stage two of its expansion: connecting up with Jordan by means of three broad corridors. When the connection is completed and the approximately 100,000 square kilometres of Jordan are also at the Palestinians' disposal, the Palestinian state will cover an area of about 130,000 square kilometres.

Another 2,000 square kilometres will consist of Areas A and B in Judea and Samaria, as defined and designated for Palestinian autonomous rule in the 1995 Oslo Interim Agreement, and Israel will open three broad strips – one in the area of Nablus, a second in the area of Ramallah and a third in the area of Hebron – which will serve as corridors connecting the Palestinian state to Jordan. At that point, the total area of the state will come to 132,000 square kilometres, almost six times the area of the State of Israel, including Area C in Judea and Samaria, which Israel will annex. The Palestinians and Jordanians will decide if their united country will be called Jordan, Jordan-Palestine or simply Palestine. But because about 70 per cent of Jordanians are already Palestinians, it is merely a matter of time before Jordan becomes Palestine, by one means or another. For some reason, the world is very anxious about the fate of the Hashemite royal family. There will be no need to remove it. It is enough that the Hashemite Kingdom becomes a constitutional monarchy for the Palestinians to agree to allow it to continue to rule, at least for the foreseeable future.

This is a reasonable and just proposal. More importantly, it represents a *viable* arrangement. Any other settlement, if it does not genuinely address the region's real long-term geographical, economic and ecological needs, will not endure, owing to intolerable population density. The explosion is simply a matter of time.

The weak point of this proposal is clearly its feasibility. Why should the Egyptians agree to throw Israel this lifeline? Why should Jordan do the same, particularly as it would almost amount to national suicide? The response, at least as far as Egypt is concerned, is that pressure can be brought to bear if the world becomes convinced that the other plans, including the Road Map, are feasible only – if at all – in the short term: even if the Palestinians get everything they are currently demanding, the Israeli–Palestinian conflict will continue to bleed and grow even worse because of a lack of sufficient territory for the Palestinians. Moreover, Egypt will not be transferring its land to Israel; it will be providing a tiny proportion of its land for the establishment of a viable state for fellow Arabs and co-religionists. Besides, this arrangement would actually contribute to Egypt's internal stability. Hamas and Islamic Jihad currently enjoy considerable support among the fundamentalist movements in Egypt, which foment unrest and seek to undermine the Egyptian regime. When the people of Gaza are finally able to stretch their legs and move out of their overcrowded sardine can, it is reasonable to assume that support for the extremist religious elements will be eroded and that the pressure on Egypt will ease off.

Many other ideas that at first appeared impracticable have been realized after public opinion became convinced of their logic and ultimately embraced them. The Palestinian state is just such an idea. Only 25 years ago, anyone in Israel who supported the concept of a Palestinian state was considered deranged or, worse, a traitor. Yossi Sarid, who was one of the first to support the idea in public, was forced to leave the Labour Party as a result. Today, the idea of a Palestinian state has been accepted even by the Likud, which in the past opposed even UN Resolution 242 and resigned from a unity government that voted to accept it. Who could believe that one day Ariel Sharon would be the bulldozer who would pave the way – and by means of unilateral disengagement – to a Palestinian state? Moreover, in the past, even the United States opposed a Palestinian state. And it was an Israeli government, that of Yitzhak Rabin, that convinced itself after the Oslo agreements to accept such a state. Now, the 'vision' of a Palestinian state is at the heart of President Bush's Road Map. If the United States, on which Egypt depends both economically and militarily, pressures Egypt to allocate a tiny part of its unpopulated desert – a part unlikely to be populated by the Egyptians themselves in the foreseeable future – to its fellow Arabs, this idea will start to make sense to world public opinion, which has got used to supporting a Palestinian state only at Israel's expense.

The same goes for Jordan. Although the situation

there is more complex, public opinion can be inured even to the idea of making Jordan part of a Palestinian state. This is certainly true for the government if the right pressure is applied. In any case, the argument stands that Israel cannot accommodate a viable Palestinian state without destroying itself, and so others must make Palestinian statehood possible elsewhere.

3 INTERIM ARRANGEMENTS AND CONFLICT MANAGEMENT

Uzi Arad

In the story of Alexander the Great and the Gordian knot, King Gordius of Phrygia used to tie together the staves of his oxcart, which he then placed by the Temple of Zeus in Gordium. The knot became of importance because the oracle at Delphi foretold that he who untied the knot would rule all Asia. Many tried to undo the intricate knot, and failed. When Alexander the Great reached Asia Minor and arrived at Gordium in 333 BC, he took up the challenge, but became frustrated. Yet instead of giving up, he stepped back, called out 'What does it matter how I loose it?', drew his sword and in one bold stroke cut the knot. Ever since, the story has served to justify the notion that bold and audacious action can sometimes resolve a problem previously considered to be unsolvable.

In most cases, however, simplifying complex problems does not yield durable and stable solutions. This is why Shakespeare praised Henry V for his ability to 'unloose' the Gordian knot, not for cutting or chopping it. And certainly the use of a sword in the story should not suggest that forcible solutions can undo what other means have failed to resolve.

Understandably, fatigue with the Palestinian–Israeli stalemate seems to have aroused the desire for a Gordian solution among important Israelis and external actors.

Thus, the Geneva Accord protagonists aspire to leapfrog the tortuous negotiating process and seal a comprehensive final status agreement between Israel and the Palestinians. Now, Israel's Prime Minister Sharon has also set forth a simple and tempting option of unilateral disengagement, one which appears to require no assistance to implement. In fact, each approach fails to deal with the intricacies of the complex situation facing both Israelis and Palestinians.

The logic of the approach posited here is to avoid the pitfalls of the quick fix and ambiguous deal-making.

The shortcomings of the Geneva Accord

It would be very satisfactory to leapfrog the negotiating process and accomplish a comprehensive and final peace agreement with the Palestinians. In effect, the Geneva Accord is an attempt to demonstrate that the ingredients for such a resolution are available. But that very exercise demonstrates why such a leap is not feasible. For example, although negotiated under laboratory conditions and in a simulated format, it is basically flawed at both ends of the process. At one end, the accord does not provide a definitive resolution of the issues in dispute. A strategic 'historical' solution has to be based on each side forgoing – and not merely putting into abeyance – a cardinal goal that served as a real source of the conflict. The Right of Return is such a goal for the Palestinians, as is Greater (Eretz) Israel for the Jewish side.

The Geneva Accord clearly cedes Jewish claims on the entire Eretz Israel west of the Jordan. But it allows the

Palestinians an ideological face-saver with regard to the Right of Return, ostensibly converting it into the Right of Choice (an act of informed choice according to the wording of the accord) for the refugees plus 'acceptance of responsibility' on the part of Israel. The link to the Right of Return is oblique but present, in the reference to 'relevant clauses of the Beirut Arab League Resolution of 28 March 2002' as one of the bases of the accord. The Beirut resolution in turn refers clearly to UN General Assembly Resolution 194 of 1948 as a basis for resolving the issue. Article 11 of the resolution (which accords what has become known as 'the right of return' to all refugees willing to live in peace) is the historical bone of contention with respect to the refugee problem, and is even referred to directly in the chapter of the Geneva accord dealing with refugees. Israel's responsibility is implicit in the articles dealing with property compensation (it must pay a lump sum based on the aggregate value of Palestinian property multiplied by an economic factor) and compensation for refugee status (to which it must contribute). It is of interest that balancing Israeli claims (for example, compensation to Jewish refugees from Arab countries for lost, confiscated or destroyed property and to Israel for damage incurred as a result of the state of war), which could have been raised, are not mentioned in the accord.

This convoluted effort at finessing the refugee issue guarantees that it will remain disputed and that, more likely than not, it will involve the parties in an ongoing dispute over contending interpretations and claims rather than offer a final settlement of all outstanding issues. The same is true for the issue of Jerusalem, which is just as complex and perhaps even more sensitive and whose treatment in the Geneva Accord also almost guarantees continuous friction and a lasting need for arbitration.

At the other end of the process lies the question of how to get from here to there. Nothing in the Geneva Accord resolves the thorny issues that have plagued all efforts to move the negotiating process from the stalemate of the past few years. The complicity of the Arafat regime in acts of terrorism, and the presence of terrorists within Fatah's own ranks as well as in the Islamist groups Hamas and the Palestinian Islamic Jihad, present an almost insurmountable obstacle to a negotiating process that would lead to a real, as opposed to a hypothetical, final status agreement. Furthermore, neither the Palestinian Authority nor the Israeli government has expressed support for or commitment to proceeding on the basis of the Geneva Accord.

Therefore, the basic question is whether resuming the negotiation process between Israel and the Palestinians is possible at this juncture. (Security cooperation is another matter, as discussed below.) The fact that the conflict is not ripe for resolution, even following the replacement of Arafat by Mahmoud Abbas, harms the parties' ability to begin negotiations as well as the prospects for reaching a final status agreement. Moreover, the loss of credibility on both sides and the apparent incapacity of the Palestinian side to undertake authoritative commitments reduce the likelihood of relaunching the negotiation process.

The unilateral disengagement option

Against this backdrop, the option of unilateral measures has been gaining ground among Israeli decision-makers, reflecting their sense of futility concerning the prospects of resuming the negotiation process. Israel's Prime Minister Sharon articulated the rationale for this change of course in his original presentation of the disengagement idea at the Herzliya Conference on National Security in December 2003. He described his resort to unilateral initiatives as a default position, arguing that had there been a viable and performing partner, he would have preferred to pursue the Road Map process. However, disarray in the Palestinian camp and the posture of the Palestinian Authority made it impossible to embark upon even Phase I of the Road Map. That, he argued, left Israel with no choice but to search for an alternative course of action that would increase the sense of security among Israelis and not depend on the Palestinians.

The Sharon initiative for unilateral disengagement is based on the completion of the security fence around the West Bank (but incorporating major Jewish settlement areas). It will include evacuation of the Gaza Strip (with or without Israeli control of the border between the Gaza Strip and Egypt at Rafah) and several isolated settlements in the northern part of the West Bank.

This initiative does not, however, constitute a purely unilateral act, unlike previous instances when Israel has moved energetically on a unilateral course of action, either militarily or diplomatically, with varying degrees of success. The Israeli government has commenced negotiations with the US over the plan and the line of the security fence. Sharon and his senior staff have also sought to receive from the US administration certain political gains, such as endorsement of the security fence and a declaration that negotiations between Israel and the Palestinians would not have to resume pending a leadership change in the Palestinian camp.

That leadership change has now occurred, revealing how hazardous is the focus on diplomacy with Washington. The United States takes into consideration the positions of its Quartet partners, particularly the EU, and may need to reach an understanding with the EU over the Israeli–Palestinian issue as part of its efforts to agree on a common agenda for the Greater Middle East. The EU, in turn, will certainly take into account Palestinian interests.

Israel is thus being asked to address Palestinian interests and will end up dealing both directly and indirectly with the Palestinian partner that Sharon said did not exist when he launched his initiative. The minuet of contacts and negotiations will not end there. The Egyptians and Jordanians are intensively engaged by all the parties with respect to the Sharon initiative and its future implementation. Egypt's and Jordan's respective positions already manifest their own strong interests at stake in these issues. Moreover, a full withdrawal from the Gaza Strip might even require reopening the 1979 Egyptian–Israeli peace treaty in order to allow the stationing of more Egyptian soldiers along the border near Rafah.

Consequently, and contrary to its touted unilateralism, the Sharon initiative is bound to result in an arrangement with a larger number of participants than that prescribed by the Road Map. Usually, increasing the number of parties in a specific framework of negotiations is bound to reduce the likelihood of achieving a negotiated arrangement.

Thus, what has been described as a fundamentally unilateral initiative – whose presumed simplicity and self-reliant character explain its attractiveness to the Israeli public – has turned into a highly complex set of unstructured multilateral concepts and negotiations with a commensurate set of conditionalities and inter-dependencies.

It seems, then, that there is no real room for pure unilateralism when it comes to this issue. A purely unilateral approach would backfire by alienating the United States and thereby undermine the stability of whatever arrangements Israel is seeking to accomplish through its own means. In addition, there is significant room for low-key negotiation even when it appears that the time is not ripe for full-fledged formal negotiations.

However, in the event that the disengagement initiative is pursued and the negotiation process is deferred, Israel will face a problem of conflict management: how to implement the policy without further destabilization and escalation. Then the effort should be on managing some form of coordination and understandings, tacit or overt, between Israel and the Palestinians. In addition, both sides should also deal with the management of daily life and seek practical solutions at the local level.

A long-term framework for conflict management and resolution

A purely unilateral course by Israel is, as indicated above, not feasible. Unilateralism could instead be incorporated into a conflict-management process based on the Road Map. This process would take place within a restructured and incremental framework of long-term negotiations that would take into account political feasibility and lead eventually to a resolution of the conflict. Such a framework, phased over the next decade, could integrate a short-term unilateral approach of approximately a year.

This time-frame may seem excessive to some. However, the lessons of previous attempts, as well as present conditions and circumstances, point to the need for a longer period than was optimistically stipulated by the Oslo Process and the Road Map to prepare the ground for a final status agreement and a resolution of the outstanding issues. As suggested, a plausible work plan can be conceived in terms of a decade and possibly more. This is because, among other reasons, some of the necessary political conditions for a successful and durable solution to the conflict may take years to materialize.

Even the Geneva Accord – the simulated negotiation of a final status agreement, which received an unusually high degree of visibility – revealed to spectators how fragile the ground is and how much it was an exercise in virtual reality and in futility. This exercise was an effort to telescope in time what probably would require long and arduous negotiation sessions. It demonstrated that behind the façade of agreement linger profound areas of disagreement. On certain cardinal issues of permanent status, especially Jerusalem and refugees, neither societies nor their governments are yet ready to find common ground. The fact, therefore, that no negotiating process has started and that so many issues were papered over suggests that more time will indeed be required. One simply cannot accept a hypothetical simulation exercise or an attempt to escape into the future that ignores the exigencies and circumstances on the ground.

Time is also required to achieve the conditions, particularly Palestine's political transformation and institution-building, which are essential for a true, real and lasting construct of peace. Given that progress is in the interest of both parties but that a comprehensive settlement is nowhere in sight, we should focus our attention on effective conflict management as we proceed towards conflict resolution.

In the Israeli–Palestinian context, conflict management would have two aspects. The first would be the effort to resolve issues gradually, in a phased approach. This is the logic of the sequential or phased approach that has been at the basis of both the Oslo process and the Road Map. Common to both approaches has been the belief that progress towards peace should be accomplished in pre-defined phases, each building upon the previous one, and spread over a defined time-line measured in years.

The second aspect of conflict management is the need to contain and manage a conflict pending its full resolution and even while the parties execute semi-coordinated unilateral measures in order to prevent escalation. That presupposes greater governance capacities and authority on the Palestinian side. In other words, effective conflict management demands Palestinian political transformation and institution-building if the process is to lead to a durable agreement providing for a viable, independent, secure, sovereign and democratic Palestinian state as envisaged by the Road Map. Moreover, Palestinian political transformation, entailing the internalization of democratic values and principles, could enhance the evolution of political ripeness on both sides.

Political change, let alone institution-building and political transformation, is a process that cannot be accomplished instantly. Europeans, more than Americans, will certainly appreciate this point. For example, the process of European integration, which was conceived in the 1950s, has taken 50 years to produce an identifiable half-way point between a state-centred system and a possibly fully integrated one. But, more interestingly, the reason why such a profound process of political change was successfully set in motion is that it was not meant to be accomplished in one bold stroke. Of course, one could have produced a hypothetical design for a federated Europe. However, the process of reaching this destination has necessitated a process that evolves one step at a time, with each step leading to the next while placing reasonable milestones on the way and providing for sufficient lead times and intervals so that diplomacy and political work can overcome resistance and build momentum for change.

In some ways, achieving a political resolution of the Arab–Israeli and Palestinian–Israeli conflicts is no less complex and requires overcoming more difficult hurdles than establishing, say, a common European currency and bank, processes that took decades to accomplish. The Palestinian Israeli conflict cannot be disconnected from the Israeli–Arab conflict in general or from the domestic considerations of neighbouring Arab countries. No Israeli–Palestinian final agreement will be stable as long as radical elements in the Arab world and Iran attempt to derail it though terrorism. Therefore, the assumption that agreement between Israel and a legitimate Palestinian counterpart will suffice is naïve. The refugee problem and questions of security both derive from the inclusion of the rest of the region in the settlement and those parties' acquiescence in the end of the conflict.

A further consideration is that democratic practices, values and traditions have been absent in the Palestinian body politic, as in all other Arab countries. There are prospects of redressing this deficit, although to succeed the Palestinians will have to demonstrate greater commitment than is apparent in other parts of the Arab world. Yet the Palestinians are in a relatively poor position compared with other Arab states in the region: they have no proven governance capabilities and their economy has no firm and independent basis, in terms of either resources or investment potential; it cannot compare even with the Syrian or Jordanian economies. In other words, the viability of a Palestinian democracy is questionable, as is the Palestinian Authority's ability to undergo political transformation unless there is a major effort sustained by international support and guidance and managed by an effective Palestinian leadership. Again, if we are to look at recent European experience, the political transformation of the central and east European countries after the Cold War took almost 15 years, even though their starting point in the early 1990s was comparatively better by far. Only against this backdrop can one really appreciate how formidable the process is that the Palestinians are expected to undergo.

Nevertheless, the situation may be even graver if one considers that, left to its own devices, a Palestinian state is quite likely to become a failed state the moment it declares independence, requiring an emergency rescue operation in the form of an international trusteeship. In that respect, the idea of a trusteeship is not just an interim measure between present-day Israeli occupation and future independence and statehood. Rather, the international community often considers trusteeship to be a solution for salvaging states that have gained independence but have not become viable, beginning instead to drift and collapse into the now recognized syndrome of state failure.

Be that as it may, the necessities of effective conflict management, as well as political feasibility, the lack of economic and political viability and the likely need for a trusteeship all imply that time will be needed and that no leapfrogging into impractical futures is possible. Therefore, the parties should adjust previously negotiated phased schemes to the present political and security circumstances and constraints and revise the phases, the sequence and the time required to fit what can realistically be achieved.

The essence of the policy

A restructured process, drawing on past experience and proposals and extending over a decade, could consist of the following elements.

The preliminary phase. This phase would see the creation of the necessary conditions for entry into Phase I of the Road Map. In it, both sides would undertake semi-coordinated unilateral steps in order to position themselves to perform the agreed undertakings of the Road Map's Phase I. On the Palestinian side, this would entail primarily political and security consolidation and possibly a negotiated truce observed by all Palestinian armed groups. Israel, for its part, would complete the fence without prejudice to future territorial negotiations, dismantle remote settlements and outposts, disengage and redeploy its forces from areas where the Palestinians take restraining action against terrorists, and assist through economic and other measures Palestinian entry into the Road Map process. Israel would continue to retain full control of the Palestinian Authority's external borders. This phase could well run into 2006. The measures in this phase should be pursued primarily at the pace that the political traffic can bear. Although some of these steps, particularly action against terror, are part and parcel of Phase I of the Road Map, their inclusion at this stage could allow greater flexibility to the parties before they enter the stricter, performance-based modalities of the rest of the Road Map.

The second phase. This phase could be the equivalent of the Road Map's Phase I. Although some of the measures incorporated in the Road Map were to have been executed previously, most of the measures would come after the initial and minimal consolidation of the Palestinian Authority's capacity to govern, as noted above. Therefore, the second, restructured phase would involve major and substantive measures, ranging from fully-fledged Palestinian institution-building and leadership change to an extensive crackdown on the armed militias and terrorist infrastructures, including their dismantlement, so that the Palestinian Authority would be able to assume the responsibilities of statehood (presumably in the next phase). These tasks would demand considerable time.

It might well turn out that these measures and others, including those required of Israel, cannot be telescoped into one overloaded phase. Consequently, breaking down this phase into two or three consecutive sub-phases, each one with a detailed plan of action that would take into account political will and feasibility, could enhance the prospects for successful progress. The Road Map's rush to accomplish the substantial measures specified in its Phase I, the sooner to reach the subsequent phases, reflects the superficiality with which many of the truly formidable tasks required are treated. This superficiality has contributed much to undercutting the Road Map's seriousness of purpose and to its delay, if not evident failure. If approached more methodically, this vital phase could last several years.

It is in this period that a Palestinian failure to perform

may require a massive international response. In fact, should the Palestinians not be able to deliver tangible results, and if Israel is expected to carry out further redeployments, then the only credible alternative to paralysis would be the insertion of a US-led international force capable of relieving Israel of its counter-terrorism burden and substituting for what the Palestinian security forces were expected to accomplish. A similar failure by the Palestinians to deliver on institution-building and leadership change would necessitate a parallel international involvement to relieve them of these obligations. Thus, a full-fledged trustee regime might have to be instituted in the event of a failure by the Palestinian Authority to deliver on requirements stipulated in Phase I of the Road Map.

The third and fourth phases. The substance of the next stage would borrow from the rationale of the Road Map's Phase II. That is, a mid-process pause and a period of transitional Palestinian statehood are needed before that state is offered its full territorial expanse, to be sure that it is able to assume its responsibilities. The initial phase of transitional statehood may follow on from a period of trusteeship, in which case it should allow for the orderly transfer of authority from the trustees to a Palestinian government. But this phase and the following one should also incorporate other critical aspects that are addressed only cursorily in the Road Map.

Notably, the Israeli–Palestinian process should clearly not remain detached from its regional context for too long. With the passing of time, progress is to be expected on other regional issues which, in turn, should facilitate progress on the Palestinian track as well. These regional developments may include the stabilization and eventual democratization of the adjacent Arab countries; revival of the multilateral tracks conceived under the Madrid process, so as to provide for more options and greater flexibility in addressing final status issues on the Israeli–Palestinian agenda; and even possible peace negotiations with Syria and Lebanon. Hopefully, with the possible stabilization of Iraq, new opportunities will present themselves for resolving final status issues in a regional context.

It should be mentioned at this juncture that neither the Road Map nor the Oslo process called for action on the refugee issue. However, this matter was discussed by a working group as part of the Madrid multilateral track. The introduction of an internationally organized multilateral regional regime on refugees, whether in connection with a trusteeship or not, could be an appropriate vehicle for more effective management of this issue. The tendency to put the main onus for the refugee problem on Israel (along with some non-Arab countries which are expected to accept refugees) is a reflection of the Arabs' refusal to absorb refugees into the fabric of their own fragile societies, as in the case of Lebanon and the Gulf states. The democratization of these countries, providing for a de-tribalization of local politics, may facilitate a new outlook regarding acceptance of people who are already the second generation living in those countries.

Reaching the fourth and final phase of the process, that of concluding and implementing the final status agreement based on a two-state formula, will take place on a timescale measured in years and resembling processes in Europe. The contours of this final agreement might be different from those conceived under the limitations of current conditions. The passage of time, along with the social, political and economic changes that are certain to evolve in Palestinian society and in the region, could suggest new formulae for accomplishing what remains the historically valid formula for resolving the Israeli–Palestinian dispute – partitioning historical Palestine between both parties.

Within this context, regional geopolitical conditions will considerably affect the final status. At this stage, the parties should consider incorporating additional factors into their equation. With the final partition of historical Palestine, both sides should address the future of the Israeli Arab population, particularly that element residing in areas adjacent to the new Palestinian state. Should demography be a key factor in the partition, as it was in most partition plans throughout the twentieth century, the much debated land exchanges between the Palestinian state and Israel may also include those Israeli Arab localities adjacent to the Palestinian state. Another demographic issue would be the constitutional relationship between Jordan and the Palestinian state. As the majority of Jordan's population is Palestinian, overlooking this matter in the final status arrangements would not seem to contribute to regional stability.

Conclusion

The fundamental shortcoming of both the Road Map and the simulated exercise of the Geneva Accord is the assumption that the conflict can be resolved as of now, in a single stroke. There can be no 'instant peace'. Similarly, the purely unilateral approach is not feasible either. Therefore, the process prescribed in the Road Map and the lessons of the Israeli–Palestinian process so far require a longer-term, multilateral and incremental process of conflict management leading to resolution. The absence of political ripeness, the lack of credibility and political feasibility, and the incapacity of the Palestinian Authority currently raise the likelihood that both parties could execute a series of coordinated unilateral measures in the short term. If properly managed, and assuming that the political circumstances would allow it, this course of action could facilitate steady if tedious progress towards resumption of the negotiation process in a phased framework over the next decade. Such a process leading to a two-state solution cannot do without the necessary political transformation, institution-building, leadership changes and security reforms on the Palestinian side. Any agreement that attempts to shorten this process is doomed to fail.

Achieving a lasting resolution of the Israeli–Palestinian conflict necessitates a more comprehensive approach to the negotiation process. The Road Map and other proposals lack a sufficient integration of fundamental elements that directly affect the conflict. They include regional processes and institutions, the Lebanese–Israeli and Syrian–Israeli negotiation tracks, and the Palestinian communities within Israel and Jordan.

The restructured phased approach proposed here takes account of realities and does not overlook the ten years or so of the Israeli–Palestinian negotiation process. It involves parallel and, where possible, coordinated steps by the parties and a much more graduated approach that uses time to effect political change.

4 INTERNATIONAL INTERVENTION FOR CONFLICT MANAGEMENT AND RESOLUTION

Joel Peters and Orit Gal

The evolving context

The collapse of the Israeli–Palestinian peace process and the escalation of violence between Israel and the Palestinians over the past four years have led to growing calls for the international community to take steps to stabilize the situation and to bring the parties back to the negotiating table. The demand for robust and sustained diplomatic engagement on the part of the international community has been accompanied recently by talk of the need for the deployment of an international peacekeeping force to reinforce any diplomatic initiatives.

The demand for international intervention and a peacekeeping force in the region has been voiced primarily by the Palestinians. The idea has received a sympathetic hearing from the international community, with several leading figures and commentators echoing Palestinian sentiments. Such sympathy, however, has yet to be translated into any real policy initiatives.

Also, until recently, the idea of an international peacekeeping force has been given short shrift by Israeli policy-makers. The stationing of foreign troops in Gaza and the West Bank was generally rejected on the grounds that this would undermine Israel's security interests, and the idea was depicted as a ploy on the part of the Palestinians to internationalize the conflict, and dismissed as a tactic aimed at imposing a political solution on the parties.

. Nonetheless, the political impasse, the seemingly endless cycle of action and reaction, and the atmosphere of suspicion and lack of trust between Israel and the Palestinians have led to a degree of debate within Israel as to the possible advantages of an international force as part of future efforts to bring about an end to the violence and to restart the peace process.

Our aim here is to contribute to that debate. We argue that the deployment of an international peace-keeping force in the West Bank and Gaza needs to be included in any future Israeli policy planning. In particular, the deployment of an international force should be considered in the context of Israel's plans to separate from the Palestinians, dismantle settlements and withdraw its forces from the West Bank and Gaza. A peacekeeping force would be entrusted with facilitating the process of an Israeli disengagement from Gaza and the West Bank; creating an effective Palestinian security capability and dismantling terrorist capabilities; assisting the Palestinian Authority and overseeing the reconstruction of the Palestinian economy, infrastructure and democratic institutions; and paving the way for the eventual establishment of a viable Palestinian state.

Discussion of the possible deployment of an international mission should not be viewed as inimical to Israel's security interests. International intervention should be seen as a measure with the potential to stabilize the current situation, underwrite any future peace process and enhance rather than weaken Israeli interests. International intervention can reinforce efforts to revive the peace process and could assist Israel in dealing with the short-, medium- and long-term security challenges that have emerged from the past four years of conflict with the Palestinians.

The idea of a third party presence in the Israeli Palestinian conflict has gained increasing credibility in recent years and has found a place on the political agenda. The Clinton Parameters of December 2000 spoke of the introduction of an international force in the wake of an Israeli withdrawal from the West Bank and Gaza, stating that 'Palestine will have an international force for border security and deterrent purposes'. International monitoring would also be deployed to oversee any agreement reached over the Temple Mount/Haram Al-Sharif. The Road Map, announced in April 2003 and endorsed by the UN Security Council in November 2003, assigns a role for outside parties. In Phase I, it proposes that 'Quartet representatives begin informal monitoring and consult with the parties on the establishment of a formal monitoring mechanism and its implementation'. With the transition to Phase II of the process, the Road Map calls for an 'enhanced international role in monitoring transition, with the active, sustained, and operational support of the Quartet', but it fails to describe what such an 'enhanced' role would entail. A third-party role is also envisioned in the Geneva Accord, which calls for an international verification group 'to facilitate, assist in, guarantee, monitor, and resolve disputes relating to the implementation of an agreement and [for] a multinational force [to] be established to provide security guarantees to the parties'.

Given that the Road Map has not been activated, calls for some form of international intervention have not gone away. Indeed, following Ariel Sharon's speech to the Herzliya Conference on National Security at the end of December 2003 announcing his plans to unilaterally withdraw Israeli forces from Gaza and the northern part of the West Bank and to dismantle all Jewish settlements in those areas, attention has turned to the need for an international force to monitor the transition in order to ensure that disorder does not erupt in the wake of Israel's departure. More importantly, following the death of Arafat and ascendance of Mahmoud Abbas to replace him, offers have been extended from various quarters (American, British and Egyptian) to assist the Palestinian Authority in resuming control and rebuilding its security forces should Israel carry out its intention to leave. Concerns about a political vacuum in Gaza have also led to calls in Israel for an international force to maintain order once it withdraws.[1]

Indeed, the original disengagement plan presented by Ariel Sharon makes reference to the potential role of a third-party presence. The plan states: 'Israel agrees that, in coordination with it, advice, aid and instruction will be given to Palestinian security forces for the purpose of fighting terror and maintaining public order by American, British, Egyptian, Jordanian or other experts, as will be agreed upon by Israel.' The plan refers to the possibility of a foreign security presence, to be coordinated

[1] See Gilad Sher, 'A Stabilizing Force Headed by the USA', *Ha'aretz*, 15 June 2003; and Pinchas Meidan-Shani, 'An International Force for Gaza,' *Ha'aretz*, 29 January 2004.

with and agreed by Israel. It also calls for 'the presence of an international body that will accept proprietorship' of the land and property assets of the settlements. The revised four-stage disengagement plan of 28 May 2004, endorsed by the Israeli government on 6 June 2004 and approved by the Knesset on 24 October 2004, states that Israel will not leave the houses of the settlements intact but speaks of Israel's aspiration to transfer the industrial and agricultural facilities of the settlements to an international third party. In addition, it refers to the creation of an international mechanism for coordination with Israel and to international bodies that will work to develop the Palestinian economy.[2]

Even so, discussions about international intervention have remained on the margin of the political and security discourse in Israel. By abstaining from serious discussion of this subject, Israel has allowed the Palestinians, the Arab states and other international detractors of Israel to determine the agenda. Such an approach does not serve Israel's interests, and the time is now ripe for examining the possibilities more seriously.

The past decade has witnessed a dramatic change in the number, scope and operational components of peace-keeping missions in conflicts around the globe. The international community has developed a comprehensive 'toolbox' for and gained a wealth of expertise in dealing with complex international crises and maintaining peace in post-conflict environments. Israeli leaders should learn from the experience of the international

---

[2] Details of the original and the revised disengagement plan can be found on the *Ha'aretz* website (*http://www.haaretzdaily.com*).

community in peacekeeping operations in other conflicts. Israel should take the initiative and play a central role in the planning, design and promotion of any future peacekeeping force. In so doing, it would ensure that its mandate reflects Israeli concerns and contributes in the best possible manner to a peaceful resolution of the conflict.

The intention here, in keeping with accompanying policy proposals, is to outline a number of assumptions and considerations that inform the argument to be developed. Consideration is then given to the parameters and the military security and civil economic components and the possible functions of an international force. Within the scope of this paper it is not possible to discuss in detail the specific mandate and force structure of a putative international peacekeeping mission, but such work has been undertaken by a number of ongoing track-two initiatives.[3]

Having addressed Israeli concerns over the deployment of a peacekeeping mission in the West Bank and Gaza and suggested ways for allaying those fears, we set out the basic argument for an international peacekeeping force as an Israeli policy option and discuss the

[3] See Jarat Chopra and Jim McCallum with Amjad Atallah and Gidi Grinstein, *Planning Considerations for International Involvement in the Israeli-Palestinian Conflict Part I*; Amjad Atallah, Jarat Chopra, Yaser Dajani, Orit Gal, Jim McCallum and Joel Peters, *Planning Considerations for International Involvement in the Israeli-Palestinian Conflict Part II*; and Amjad Atallah, Jarat Chopra, Yaser M. Dajani, Orit Gal, Joel Peters and Mark Walsh, *Planning Considerations for International Involvement in an Israeli Withdrawal from Palestinian Territory.* These reports can be found at *http://www.carlisle.army.mil/usacsl/Studies.asp*. These papers are the product of a series of meetings between Israelis, Palestinians and international experts held over the past two years to discuss this question.

contribution such a mission could make in dealing with short-, medium- and long-term threats and challenges to Israel's security.

International intervention should not be seen as a policy in itself. Rather, it needs to be viewed as a tool that is integral to any future political initiatives, complemented by a broader set of measures aimed at bringing about a stable and lasting peace between Israel and the Palestinians, and addressing Israel's security concerns. We conclude by proposing a series of steps and confidence-building measures that should be considered by the international community and the Arab world in conjunction with sending an international peacekeeping force to the region.

Policy choices and preferences

The prime impetus for proposing the deployment of an international peacekeeping force in the West Bank and Gaza is to advance the prospects of a peaceful resolution of the Israeli–Palestinian conflict and to enable Israel to live in a state of peaceful coexistence with its neighbours. Peace is more than simply the absence of war. Israel at peace defines a situation in which it exists within secure and recognized boundaries and in which it is recognized as the legitimate homeland of the Jewish people, free from threat and the use of force. The foundation of any peace process and peace agreement with the Palestinians needs to be the principle of territorial compromise and the exchange of land for peace. A just and lasting resolution of the Israeli–Palestinian conflict requires the establishment of a viable Palestinian state living side by side in peace and security with Israel and its other neighbours. The achievement of peace necessitates compromise and the relinquishing of certain core values on the part of both sides. For Israel, this entails not only withdrawal from the West Bank and Gaza and the evacuation of Jewish settlements but also abandoning the idea of Jewish sovereignty over the entire Land of Israel, in particular over the biblical heartland of Judea and Samaria.

In the long run, Israel's presence in the West Bank and Gaza threatens the continued existence of Israel as a Jewish, democratic state. Maintaining Israel's rule over three million Palestinians in the West Bank and Gaza leads to inevitable tension between the preservation of the Jewish character of the state and its democratic values. If Israel remains in the West Bank and Gaza, its choices will be simple but unpalatable. To be a democracy, it will have to grant equal rights to all, thereby losing its Jewish majority. To be Jewish it will have to deprive three million Arabs of political rights, thereby forfeiting its democratic nature. Only by separation from the West Bank and Gaza can Israel remain true to both its Jewish and its democratic values.

Peace will enable Israel to reinforce its democratic and Jewish character. Since its establishment in 1948, Israel has been a nation at war; security and survival have been its primary concern. Such an environment has inevitably led to a curtailing of certain civil liberties. By the same token, peace will allow for a long-overdue public discourse about the Jewish attributes of the state and an institutionalization of the outcomes of these discussions.

A strong and secure Israel is the underlying goal of any policy, and Israel must retain its capacity to defend its citizens and borders from attack. But long-term security and stability cannot be achieved solely through self-reliance, the projection of military power and deterrence. The changing context of security – the actions of small independent groups operating outside the formal framework of the state and the targeting of civilian populations – demands new cooperative approaches and needs to be addressed in a regional context.

The strength of a country amounts to more than the aggregation of its military power. It also comprises a number of socio-economic variables, such as economic growth (which necessitates a positive investment climate), education, employment and the social welfare of its citizens. Peace will allow Israel to redirect economic resources from security needs to the socio-economic welfare of its citizens. It will also bring international and regional legitimacy and pave the way for long-term security and stability.

Assumptions about the nature and context of international intervention

Any future policy options for Israel need to relate to the current geopolitical and geostrategic context and to take into account the changes in the political and social environment that have occurred as a result of the past four years of violence.

At the most fundamental level, those years of violence have led to a breakdown in trust between Israel and the

Palestinians in the political, operational and public spheres. Prior to the outbreak of the *intifada*, Israelis and Palestinians worked closely on a variety of operational issues, especially in the field of security. There was an ongoing engagement and cooperation between the civil societies. But the violent struggle between Israel and the Palestinians has led to a re-evaluation of the nature of the conflict, the perceptions and role of civil society and the possibility of progress in the near future. In Israel, the passivity or refusal of the Palestinian Authority to constrain and take effective measures against terror activities has been interpreted as tacit endorsement of those activities and has led Israelis to believe that they are now involved in a struggle for their survival.

Throughout the Oslo process, the two-state solution (Israel for the Jews, Palestine for the Palestinians, side by side between the Mediterranean and the Jordan) was the underlying rationale of Israeli, Palestinian and international policy. This rationale seems to have been accepted by the majority of both Israelis and Palestinians. At the formal level, a two-state solution remains the intended outcome of a renewed Israeli–Palestinian peace process.

However, four years of violence have created new trends and perceptions which threaten the sustainability of this logic. Both parties now question whether the other side is striving for secure borders within the two-state solution. On the Israeli side, many are questioning the Palestinians' desire for a peaceful resolution of the conflict and their capacity to establish a stable political entity living peacefully next to Israel.

The continuing political impasse, the loss of public

confidence in the attainability of a peace agreement and structural changes on the ground such as the disintegration of the Palestinian Authority as a governing power, the construction and route of the separation fence and moves towards unilateral measures threaten the viability of a two-state solution. These trends are likely to intensify, making a bold political initiative all the more urgent and important.

International efforts to bring an end to the violence and to resume negotiations have been based on the logic of the Oslo process: interim agreements designed to boost mutual confidence and gradually pave the way for final status negotiations. However, the ongoing violence and recrimination have seen an erosion of the most basic level of trust required for this approach to be effective. The Road Map is the latest political initiative to adopt an incremental approach towards resolving the conflict. Although Israel and the Palestinians both accepted the Road Map, neither side believed in it. Interim stages were viewed not in terms of implementation but as breathing spaces in which power and political advantage could be gained. The incremental measures outlined in the first phase were viewed as providing concessions to the other side and carrying high political costs, with few gains in return.

The Israeli and Palestinian leaderships have consistently proved incapable of making long-term strategic decisions. They have focused instead on short-term manoeuvres for political gain. Devoid of an overall strategic direction, Israeli policy has become tied up with Palestinian action and been manifested as positive or negative responses to Palestinian choices. In the absence of belief in a credible partner, Israel has turned to advocating unilateral measures aimed at short-term conflict management but lacking any coherent long-term strategic vision.

The call for international intervention

Israel needs to look beyond unilateral measures and initiate a new set of ideas to revive the peace process. By itself, Israel does not possess the capacity to deal with the challenges and threats that have been wrought by the violence of the past four years. In this effort, it is in need of the active and sustained support of the international community. This support needs to look beyond renewed diplomatic efforts and requires the deployment of an international peacekeeping mission in the West Bank and Gaza. Such a peacekeeping mission, containing both military security and civilian components, would be entrusted with stabilizing the situation on the ground, assisting the Palestinians with rebuilding their governance and security capacities, serving as a catalyst for reviving the peace process, and addressing the broader conflict environment. The inclusion in Israel's strategic thinking of a peacekeeping force would mean bestowing on the international community a stake and responsibility for the emergence of a Palestinian political entity committed to peaceful coexistence with Israel.

International intervention should not be viewed as a substitute for a political process, nor can it fill a political void. The deployment of a peacekeeping force must be complementary to a political process and the resumption of negotiations between Israel and the Palestinians leading to an Israeli withdrawal from the West Bank as well as Gaza and the realization of a two-state solution to the conflict. To ensure that any third party presence obtains local and international legitimacy, a set of criteria and a shared end goal, within a specific time-frame, need to be defined from the outset. Although stabilization of the current violence is a priority for any peacekeeping mission, its mandate must be seen not as a consolidation of the status quo but as a catalyst for progress and revival of the peace process.

International intervention requires the convergence of Israeli and Palestinian expectations about the mission's strategic purpose. A peacekeeping force needs to address the strategic priorities and concerns of both sides. Any third party presence will fail, and prove to be counter-productive for prospects of long-term stability, if it is seen as ignoring the interests of one party at the expense of the other. From Israel's perspective, this would require the international force to ensure that the Palestinians honour their commitment to cease all violence and terrorism directed against Israel and its citizens, and to assist the Palestinian security apparatus in carrying out effective operations against groups engaged in terrorism and in dismantling terrorist infra-structures and capabilities. From the Palestinians' per-spective, it would require that an international presence ensure that Israel does not undermine the reconstruction of their governance capabilities, that Israel does not undertake any unilateral measures that might prevent the emergence of a viable Palestinian state and, in particular, that it abides by its commitments to freeze settlement activity until the eventual border between Israel and a Palestinian state is determined.

An international peacekeeping force cannot be imposed on the parties; it needs the prior agreement of both Israel and the Palestinians. Such a force needs to be credible and acceptable to both sides and to receive the endorsement of their respective publics. A clear understanding must be reached at the mission's outset as to the scope of its mandate and time-frame and as to possible outcomes. In the initial stage, the deployment of an international mission needs to accompany Israel's complete disengagement from Gaza, a withdrawal of its forces from Palestinian towns in the West Bank and the evacuation of settlements in order to allow for geographical contiguity and freedom of movement between Palestinian population areas. The dispatch of an international force needs to be followed by negotiations between Israel and the Palestinians over the eventual border and the potential role of the international community in the management of the border regime between Israel and a future Palestinian state.

This presumes a Palestinian interlocutor. An international peacekeeping mission cannot serve as a substitute for the Palestinians. The international mission would not take over formal control of the Palestinian territories and become the governing authority in place of the Palestinian Authority.[4] Its purpose would be to

[4] For ideas proposing that an international force take control from the Palestinian Authority and calling for the creation of an international trusteeship for the West Bank and Gaza, see Martin Indyk, 'A Trusteeship for Palestine?', *Foreign Affairs*, Vol. 82, No. 3 (May/June 2003), pp. 51–66.

prevent the total disintegration of governance within the Palestinian Authority and to avert the socio-economic collapse of the West Bank and Gaza. An international force would work in partnership with the Palestinian Authority to assist and supervise the rebuilding of its governance capacities, to ensure that it implements the necessary reforms in its security, administrative, judicial, and economic institutions, and to monitor Palestinian fulfilment of any agreements signed with Israel.

Mandate and authority

An international peacekeeping force would require a clear mandate with specific tasks and it would need to be allocated the appropriate resources and authority.[5] Its role can be divided into four interrelated functions: supervising, capacity-building and coordination, monitoring and legitimacy-building. These functions differ in their operational scope and degree of intrusiveness. The international community needs to commit itself to guiding the peace process through the following four consecutive stages: the disengagement and withdrawal of Israeli forces; rebuilding the Palestinians' governing capacity; negotiations towards permanent status arrangements; and, finally, the implementation of a peace treaty.

A clear and defined purpose from the outset would be

[5] Several of the ideas in this section are drawn from Atallah, Chopra et al., *Planning Considerations for International Involvement in the Israeli-Palestinian Conflict Part II* and Atallah, Chopra et al., *Planning Considerations for International Involvement in an Israeli Withdrawal from Palestinian Territory*. The authors would like to acknowledge the input of the co-authors of these reports into their thinking on these issues.

essential to fostering the legitimacy of the mission and to managing expectations. The appropriate force structure, resources and tasks would need to be determined and guaranteed prior to the mission's deployment. In other conflict situations, the international community has frequently adopted a policy of incremental engagement and minimal deployment, thereby limiting the capacity of the mission to effect any real change.

At the same time, expectations must not be set too high. Any international intervention demands a sustained commitment by the contributing nations in terms of both political support and material costs. Any mandate needs to reflect the resources available, the degree of political commitment of the international community to such an international mission and the risk the contributing parties are willing to take. It also needs to take into account the capacity of an international force to alter the strategic landscape of the West Bank and Gaza and to effect political, economic and social change.

A key task for the international mission would be to supervise and oversee the reform and restructuring of the Palestinian security forces, the regulation of governance of the financial sector, the re-establishment of the rule of law and the development of an independent judiciary in the Palestinian territories. There could also be a continuation of international involvement in supervising new elections and maintaining the process of constitutional and legislative reform of Palestinian institutions.

In addition, the newly formalized international presence would be responsible for the coordination and harmonization of international efforts to rebuild the capacity of Palestinian institutions and for the reconstruction of the Palestinian economy and infrastructure. This would include the training of personnel and the provision of guidance to ensure that Palestinian institutions are effective in supplying social goods and public services and that human rights are upheld in the Palestinian Authority.

The international mission would monitor compliance with agreements between Israel and the Palestinians. Further, it would monitor security cooperation between the two sides and any incitement against Israel within educational and governmental institutions and in the Palestinian media. The mission would be responsible, too, for monitoring Israeli compliance with a settlement freeze in areas that remain under Israeli control prior to a final status agreement over the borders between Israel and Palestine.

The purpose of the international mission would have to be comprehensive. It would need to deal not only with the technical and operational aspects of the conflict but also with the conflict environment as a whole. It would have to define its strategies to multiple audiences on each side: the political leaderships, the security and civil apparatuses and the general publics. A key component of reviving the peace process is regaining the confidence of the Israeli and Palestinian publics in the possibility of a peaceful settlement to the conflict. Ultimately, the real impact of any disengagement between the sides and the presence of an international force will be determined by the way in which these measures are perceived by the two publics. The international community has to develop a comprehensive strategy to this end, and it needs to incorporate this strategy into planning for an international force. This strategy would need to include civil society projects, people-to-people activities and the promotion of a broader regional dialogue between Israel and its neighbours.

Only an American-led mission or American leadership within a NATO force would be acceptable to Israel. But an international force would also need to include countries other than the United States. To gain legitimacy it would need to have a multinational character. At the same time, the balance and composition of the force would have to be based on capability rather than the desire of states to participate. Only a small group of countries, such as member states of the European Union, Canada and Australia, possess the capability to contribute to a major civilian and/or military peacekeeping force. These countries are already overstretched with commitments to peacekeeping operations ranging from Iraq and Afghanistan to the Balkans and Africa. Careful consideration would need to be given as well to the potential contribution of Egypt and Jordan to such an international mission.

The mission would need to be American-led and be headed by a strong political leader who would have maximum political independence and possess the authority to resolve disagreements and violations of agreements by the parties. The political centre of authority of the mission would have to reside with this locally based leader and not in the national capitals of the participating countries. To ensure harmonization, the head of the mission would have to be in charge of all civilians belonging to international organizations and agencies in the West Bank and Gaza in addition to the military forces deployed. International involvement in the West Bank and Gaza is very extensive and would probably increase with a renewal of the peace process. What would be required is a comprehensive approach that rationalizes the myriad international agencies and actors operating on the ground. Without this harmoni-zation of effort on the part of the international com-munity, there is a risk that individual efforts would be counter-productive to capacity-building activities for the Palestinian state. This mix of security, political, econo-mic, humanitarian and state-building elements would require a coherent structure and single coordinating authority if international involvement is to be effective.

Israeli perspectives on international intervention

Hitherto Israel has been resolute in its opposition to an international intervention and the deployment of an international peacekeeping force in the West Bank and Gaza. The stationing of international troops there is seen as harmful to its security. The very idea that foreign troops might be able to meet Israel's security needs, even partially, runs counter to the central tenet of self-reliance in its security doctrine.

The point of departure for Israel in discussions about international intervention is its experience with the

United Nations Emergency Force (UNEF) in June 1967. The sudden removal of UNEF troops from the Sinai prior to the outbreak of the Six-Day War was a defining moment in Israeli consciousness as to the capacity and willingness of an international mission to prevent aggression against Israel. The negative attitude towards international peacekeeping has been reinforced by the ineffectual role played by the United Nations Interim Force in Lebanon (UNIFIL) in fulfilling its mandate and preventing attacks on Israel by Hizbollah. On the other hand, positive experiences and contributions are largely overlooked – namely, the United Nations Disengagement Observer Force (UNDOF) on the Golan Heights, the Multinational Force and Observers stationed in the Sinai following the signing of the peace treaty between Israel and Egypt, and the Monitoring Group established in April 1996 following Operation Grapes of Wrath to monitor the application of the understanding achieved between Israel and Lebanon.

Given the mixed performance of international peace-keeping forces in other conflict zones, Israelis question the capacity of international forces to fight terrorism effectively and to take the necessary steps to prevent terror attacks against Israeli targets. In addition, stationing foreign troops in the West Bank and Gaza is seen as severely limiting Israel's freedom of operational man-oeuvre in both preventive action and retaliatory measures against potential terrorist targets. Of equal concern is that the international community would sympathize with the Palestinians and overlook Israeli security concerns. Israel does not trust the international community's willingness to pressure the Palestinians sufficiently to ensure that they would undertake fully the necessary security and administrative reforms and abide by their commitment to dismantle the terrorist infrastructures. It also doubts the resolve of the international community to stay the course, especially should there be casualties, and to commit the necessary resources and personnel to ensure the successful completion of a mission's mandate.

In Israel the discourse on international peacekeeping has focused almost exclusively on experience with classic forms of peacekeeping – namely, overseeing the separation of forces and monitoring disengagement agreements. Little attention has been given to the changing nature of peacekeeping missions in the post-Cold War era, to the contributions played by the international community in post-conflict reconstruction and to the numerous peace-maintenance operations around the world. Critics of an international intervention have depicted it as a measure responding solely to Palestinian appeals, imposed on Israel and detrimental to its interests. Yet Israel can benefit from, and needs to draw on, the wealth of experience and expertise gained by the international community in recent years. It has a shared interest in working in partnership with the international community in facilitating an orderly disengagement from the Palestinians, in preventing socio-economic collapse in the Palestinian territories and in (re)building viable and effective Palestinian security and governmental organizations.

By engaging fully in the planning of the mandate of an international peacekeeping force, its components, force structure and operational scope, Israel can best ensure that its fears and concerns are seriously addressed and that the criteria for compliance by the Palestinians and the benchmarking of success are clearly determined. Detailed preparation would also be required to ensure that the necessary coordination and liaison mechanisms between the international force and Israel are in place. Although the Israeli public has not called for international intervention, it would not necessarily be hostile to the idea, especially if it were presented as part of an overall package aimed at bringing about stability and disengagement from the Palestinians. The April 2002 and June 2003 issues of the Peace Index, a monthly poll conducted by the Tami Steinmetz Center for Peace at Tel Aviv University, found that almost half the Israeli public favoured the idea of international intervention.[6]

Widening the framework

Calling for the deployment of an international peacekeeping force in the West Bank and Gaza would mark a radical departure for Israel. It would amount to an explicit endorsement by Israel of the internationalization of the Israeli–Palestinian conflict. Such a policy shift would afford the international community a stake in promoting stability in the region and also give it a responsibility for helping to create the conditions that would enhance Israel's perceptions of its overall security.

International intervention is not a policy in itself; it

[6] For details of the polls conducted by the Steimetz Center, see *http:// spirit.tau.ac.il/socant/peace/*.

needs to be considered as part of a broader policy initiative. That policy initiative should not be confined to the immediacy of the current situation and the need to facilitate an Israeli withdrawal from the West Bank and Gaza. The introduction of a peacekeeping force can serve as a catalyst for bringing about a fundamental change for Israel in the overall conflict environment. International intervention is not without risk. The benefits of such a step need to be discernible to the Israeli public, and cannot be confined solely to inchoate arguments about the importance for Israel of the development of viable Palestinian institutions and the socio-economic development of the Palestinian territories.

The international community needs to be responsive to Israel's security concerns and, in particular, to attend to the feelings of diplomatic isolation and being under siege among the Israeli public. It must be prepared to upgrade, individually and collectively, the level of political dialogue and security cooperation with Israel. The State of Israel should be integrated fully in all institutions of the United Nations and other international organizations, and all attempts to de-legitimize its membership in those organizations need to be combated and condemned unconditionally. Europe has an important part to play. A closer, special relationship between Israel and the European Union, especially in the field of security cooperation, needs to be forged in the context of the new European Neighbourhood Policy. In a similar vein, NATO should develop a political and security dialogue with Israel, and an action plan leading to increased participation by Israel in NATO structures and its eventual membership in the alliance should be drawn up.[7]

The onus does not lie just with the international community. The Arab world also has an important role to play in this respect. The deployment of an international force would need to be accompanied by a set of measures that helps to reshape the current regional dynamics. The Arab world would need to show its acceptance of Israel as a legitimate part of the Middle East and to take concrete measures towards the normalization of relations with it. It would have to be prepared to engage with Israel in a renewed political dialogue and to resume the multilateral economic and security dialogue of the 1990s. It would be unrealistic to expect a resumption of the multilateral Arab–Israeli talks from the point at which they were suspended in 1995, and new frameworks would have to be devised to discuss future regional cooperation between Israel and the Arab world. Efforts would also need to be directed at exploring solutions to the Palestinian refugee problem. In this respect, an international mission would need to be tasked with facilitating the transfer of UNRWA (the United Nations Relief and Works Agency) services in the West Bank and Gaza to the Palestinian Authority. In addition, Israel would have to be accepted as an equal and legitimate partner of the Euro-Mediterranean Partnership (the Barcelona process), and Arab states would have to stop opposing Israel's full participation in the political and security dialogue and the imple-

[7] For a discussion of these ideas, see Rosemary Hollis, 'The Israeli–Palestinian Road Block: Can Europe make a Difference?', *International Affairs*, Vol. 80, No. 2 (2004), pp. 191–201.

mentation of economic and civil society projects within the Barcelona framework.

The adoption of these steps would serve as an important confidence-building measure and inject new faith in the peace process. It would signal to Israel and its public that the resolution of the Israeli–Palestinian conflict forms part of a comprehensive peace between Israel and its neighbours and that the compromises it will have to undertake for peace would lead to Israel's acceptance in the Middle East and to a significant improvement in the country's standing in the international community.

Conclusion

International intervention is not without risk and cost to Israel. But that cost needs to be appraised in relation to the price of inaction, to other policy alternatives, and to the benefits such a course would bring for Israel. The Israeli public is demanding new ideas and bold initiatives to break the political impasse. A withdrawal from the West Bank and Gaza responds to Israelis' desire for disengagement and separation from the Palestinians. But a unilateral and uncoordinated Israeli withdrawal threatens to leave a political and security vacuum and would result in the further erosion of the socio-economic and living conditions of the Palestinians.

International intervention will not bring about a resolution of the Israeli–Palestinian conflict. But the introduction of an international peacekeeping force would allow for the gradual rebuilding of trust between Israel and the Palestinians, the orderly management of an Israeli withdrawal from the West Bank and Gaza, and the reconstruction and development of effective Palestinian governing institutions. In short, an international force could begin to address the political and security challenges arising from the past four years of violence.

The dispatch of an international peacekeeping force would also pose risks and political costs to the international community. The handful of countries that are capable of providing the necessary civilian and military assets are already overstretched in attending to other conflict situations, most notably Afghanistan and Iraq. Yet the current political environment, the breakdown of trust between the Israelis and the Palestinians, and the need to rebuild the Palestinian Authority's governing capacity demand a more robust response by the international community than simply re-engaging in a diplomatic process. In the current political environment, international involvement is critical for securing the conditions for an orderly Israeli withdrawal from Palestinian territories. If the international community is not responsive to Israel's input on the deployment of an international mission to facilitate and underwrite such a withdrawal, then Israel will disengage unilaterally, regardless of the potentially destabilizing consequences of such an act.

However, international intervention, if carefully planned and judiciously introduced, can make a valuable contribution to the stabilization of the current situation. It can help to move Israel and the Palestinians back along the path to a peaceful settlement and a realization of the vision of a two-state solution to their conflict.

5 UNILATERAL DISENGAGEMENT

Dan Schueftan

The essence of the policy

Unilateral disengagement is a policy designed to sever Israel from the Palestinians in the West Bank and Gaza Strip along a line unilaterally determined by Israel and following the demographic divide by means of a physical barrier to be constructed on this line. Israel will gradually pull out of the territories on the Palestinian side of that barrier and remove its settlements there. Palestinians wishing to cross the barrier into Israel will have to produce documentation and undergo a security check similar to those required when crossing other international gateways.

In the final state of the unilateral phase, Israel will leave the populated heartland of the West Bank and all of the Gaza Strip, retaining and incorporating under its control three major settlement blocks, East Jerusalem and a strip along the river Jordan and the Dead Sea. Most of the Jewish *settlers*, about three-quarters of them, will stay under Israeli control; most of the *settlements* and outposts, more than one hundred, will be dismantled or relocated either behind the pre-1967 lines (primarily in Galilee and the Negev) or to the retained settlement blocks.

The Palestinians will be left with a contiguous area both in the West Bank and the Gaza Strip. In the

Jerusalem area, complicated passages will be constructed to accommodate the Israeli requirement for an east–west link as well as the Palestinian requirement for a north–south link. In the unilateral stage, Israel will maintain strict security controls over the external borders of the Palestinian territories or find alternative arrangements for trustworthy non-Palestinian control.

The Palestinians may unilaterally declare a state, which will be instantly recognized by most countries (possibly even by the EU). Israel will not recognize it as a sovereign state until final status negotiations determine its permanent borders, satisfy Israel on the subject of security (demilitarization and other restrictions on Palestinian sovereignty) and recognize Israel as a *Jewish* nation-state. Israel will not formally annex the settlement blocks under its control but will continue to develop these areas as if they were a part of Israel, subject to restrictions agreed between Israel and the United States.

At a later stage, within or outside the context of a permanent settlement, Israel could, at its discretion, consider redefining the borders of greater Jerusalem, excluding portions heavily populated by Arabs even if they are within the post-1967 municipal boundaries and incorporating portions heavily populated by Jews (and adjacent unpopulated land) even if they were not within these boundaries (for example, Ma'ale Adumim and Giv'at Zeev – see Maps 2 and 3).

If and when the Palestinians are willing and able to negotiate a compromise settlement, Israel will be prepared to discuss permanent international borders. The route of these borders and the extent of the limitations on Palestinian sovereignty will depend largely on the length of time before the negotiations begin and the quality and credibility of assurances the Palestinians can provide for their irrevocable abandonment of the national strategy of terror. The final status agreement will also depend on unequivocal Palestinian public acceptance of the legitimacy of a *Jewish* nation-state within the borders that will be agreed upon, alongside the Palestinian *Arab* nation-state. As long as the Palestinians refuse to negotiate such a permanent settlement, the boundaries of the unilateral disengagement will persist, subject solely to unilateral Israeli decisions on further disengagement (for example in Jerusalem, as noted above).

The origins and rationale of the policy

The unilateral component

Unlike other Israeli policy options, unilateral disengagement from the Palestinian population in the occupied territories depends almost exclusively on Israeli decisions and American concurrence. A negotiated settlement, whether permanent or interim, requires Arab consent, perpetuation of the status quo rests on Arab acquiescence, and even international intervention presumably aims to coerce the parties into some kind of reciprocal arrangement. By contrast, the disengagement discussed here is indeed unilateral, at least in the sense that it does not entail political negotiations. Of course, Israel may discuss portions of this policy with the EU and the UN, carry out operative consultations with Egypt and Jordan on specific security components, and even coordinate implementation with selected Palestinians. However, unilateral disengagement will be pursued regardless of Palestinian opposition to or European criticism of some of its most essential components. Core portions of this policy are to be negotiated only with the United States.

It is, therefore, Israeli perceptions, choices and decisions that should be the focus when this option is examined. American policies can be expected to have a major effect, and European, Arab and Palestinian responses need to be considered when deliberating about its feasibility, outcome, benefits and costs. Nonetheless, the point of departure of this analysis is the Jewish majority in Israel.

The limited choice of options

The confrontation between Israel and the Palestinians has already passed the stage at which all options remain possible (let alone feasible). As far as mainstream Israelis are concerned, the traumatic experience of the past decade and a half virtually excludes two major options: mutually agreed 'peace' with the kind of national leadership that currently enjoys popular support among the Palestinians (Abu Mazen as well as Arafat), on the one hand, and perpetuated Israeli control of most of the West Bank and Gaza Strip, on the other. Both have become equally discredited among mainstream Jews in Israel. A fringe of about 15–20 per cent on each end of the political spectrum still clings to these fantasies, but opinion polls indicate a solid majority in the broad centre consistently expresses the conviction that they should no longer be seriously considered.

After decades of indecision and escapism, main-stream Israelis seem to have made up their mind. Their government may be split, hesitant and indecisive and the prime minister may be torn between his ideological commitments and his realistic assessment of the situation, even after his revolutionary public commitment to unilateral disengagement in Gaza. But the nation is ripe to pursue the only course that will enable Israel to determine its future independently of the Palestinians. Strange as it may seem, Israel needs to assert its independence and secure its right of self-determination not much less than do the Palestinians. Although both peoples have denied this right to each other, Israel is strong enough to exercise it unilaterally if and when it comes to the conclusion that all other options have been exhausted.

For about a third of a century, Israelis did not feel threatened with regard to their self-determination. Most believed since the Six-Day War that Israel could deal with the West Bank and Gaza Strip in one of two ways. The first was to incorporate these territories into Israel, or otherwise maintain strategic control over them, and settle Jews in them while offering the Palestinians self-governing autonomy of one sort or another. The second was to offer Jordan (of which the West Bank had been part before 1967) or the Palestinians (who lived there) a 'territorial compromise' in the context of a peace treaty so that the bulk of the territory and the overwhelming majority of the population would come under Arab demilitarized sovereignty, with only a few major settlement blocks to be incorporated into Israel. It is only in the past few years that most Israelis of diverse political convictions have seemingly realized that both options are no longer possible, if they ever were.

The end of the 'Greater Israel' option

Since the *intifada* of the late 1980s, mainstream Israelis have come to realize that Palestinian acquiescence in permanent Israeli control of the occupied territories is no longer attainable. Israel may be strong enough to hold on to them militarily and perhaps also determined enough to withstand international criticism, but the mood of Israeli society has changed to such an extent that domestic constraints, rather than external pressures, have become decisive and have made this option increasingly unrealistic. These constraints do not stem from a fear of *failure* to incorporate the territories into Israel but rather from a fear of the demographic and political consequences of its *success*.

The final blow came when both 'right-wing' prime ministers, Benjamin Netanyahu and Ariel Sharon, who were elected to halt the excessive concessions offered by the 'left-wing' governments of prime ministers Yitzhak Rabin, Shimon Peres and Ehud Barak, acquiesced in the partition of *Eretz Israel*. Sharon's acceptance of the establishment of a Palestinian state became politically significant in the wake of his landslide victory in the 2003 elections. That triumph came not only *in spite* of his rejection of the hardline position of the Likud central committee on this matter but most probably *because* he overruled their opposition to a Palestinian state. The last nail in the coffin of the 'Greater Israel' option was put in place by Sharon's explicit commitments to wholesale unilateral withdrawal from the Gaza Strip and a massive removal of Israeli settlements.

In spring 2004, Sharon mistakenly believed that the overwhelming public support for his disengagement initiative, together with presidential endorsement by the United States, would both deliver the Likud's *voters* and secure the support of its *registered members*. In early May 2004, he called a referendum of his party's 190,000 registered members, and his Gaza disengagement plan was defeated by a 60/40 margin. But despite a revolt in his party and the breakup of the ruling coalition, Sharon stayed the course of unilateral disengagement and maintained a 60 per cent approval rating for his policy among Likud voters as well as in the general public.

Disenchantment with 'peace'

The other option – 'peace' based on a historical compromise – lost the support of mainstream Israelis once they came to the view, in the late 1990s or at the beginning of the new millennium, that there is no real partner for such compromise on the Arab side. The Jordanian partner disengaged in the late 1980s and was eliminated by the Oslo process a few years later. The local and less radical Palestinian leadership which could have emerged in the wake of the first *intifada* lost its chance when the Rabin government handed all the assets and powers to Arafat and his radical Tunis cohorts.

In seven years of negotiations and confrontation with Israel, the Palestinian leadership proved committed to a policy of rejecting the legitimacy of the Jewish nation-state and seeking to undermine it through its insistence on the so-called Right of Return of the Palestinian refugees of 1948. It also proved to be unable and unwilling to abandon terrorism as the cornerstone of the Palestinian national strategy and instead deliberately preserved the option of terrorism as an ever-present threat.

This characterization of the Palestinian leadership is, of course, challenged by the Palestinians themselves and by the Israeli architects of the Oslo process, but what counts for practical political purposes is the perception of mainstream Jews. These Israelis gradually and reluctantly came to the conclusion that Arafat and the Palestinian leadership never intended to terminate the conflict with Israel, abandon terrorism and stop their persistent attempt to undermine the Jewish nation-state.

Israeli mistakes, inadequacies and miscalculations aside, the broad mainstream came to be convinced that this Palestinian leadership is not, and cannot be, a credible partner for peace and compromise. Most of those who were uncertain in the 1990s realized at the time of Camp David in 2000 and at the Taba talks in December–January 2000/01 that even dramatic concessions, far beyond the Israeli national consensus, are irrelevant to this Palestinian strategy. The ensuing four years of war and intensive Palestinian terrorism have taken this conviction a major step forward, to a conclusion that seems to have changed fundamentally the relations between the Israeli and Palestinian peoples.

Israeli perceptions of the Palestinian people

It is almost impossible to overestimate the impact that Palestinian terrorism has had on the perceptions of mainstream Israelis concerning the Palestinian *people* in general and the nature of future relations with it in particular. Far beyond the rage over Israeli casualties and the public debate over the appropriate measures to be taken against the terrorist onslaught, Israelis were exposed to norms of Palestinian society so alien to their own and to what they had expected that they raised questions about the very feasibility of peaceful coexistence.

Until the start of the so-called *al-Aqsa intifada* in 2000, most Israelis accepted the convenient dichotomy between, on the one hand, Islamic 'extremists', who seek to kill Jews and destroy Israel, and, on the other hand, mainstream Palestinian 'moderates' who accept Israel. The war gradually convinced them that the confrontation was more about the survival of Israel than about the fate of the occupied territories. Moreover, it became evident that the enemy was not confined to a small minority of fanatic Hamas and Islamic Jihad fighters, nor even to Arafat and the Palestinian Authority.

If one had to pick the critical turning point, it would be the lynching of two Israeli reservists who in October 2000 strayed into Ramallah, to hysterical cheers of a large crowd in the town square. The conviction of a general Palestinian enmity hardened when overwhelming evidence accumulated concerning the attitude of the Palestinian people at large towards the suicide bombers, who targeted innocent Jewish civilians in Israeli population centres. Widespread parental endorsement of

107

Palestinian children's reverence for those terrorists as role models may have had the greatest impact on Israeli perceptions. The frequent use of teenagers and some women as suicide bombers, the adulation of these mass murderers by Palestinian society and the pervasive abuse of children as human shields seemed incomprehensible, not to say hideous, to mainstream Israelis.

The immense popularity of terrorist acts against the Jewish civilian population, both before Israel took radical countermeasures and after its reoccupation of Palestinian population centres, convinced many Israelis that a political settlement was no longer an option. For such a settlement to work, Israel would need not only a partner *leadership* which is willing and able to compromise (unlike Arafat at Camp David and Taba) but also a partner *people* which will abhor the deliberate mass killing of innocent civilians as a political instrument. More important than even those two preconditions, Israel would need a partner people which is determined not to devastate its own society, affecting it for many years, perhaps for generations, even when terrorism seems to offer a transient advantage in political confrontation with an external enemy.

The Oslo process and the negotiations with the Palestinians in the 1990s began on the assumption that their national leadership and elites had learned the lessons of the 1930s and 1940s and were determined not to revisit the catastrophic policies that repeatedly brought national tragedy on their suffering people. Challenged by critics of the Oslo process about the possibility that unilateral Israeli concessions would only encourage the Palestinians to stick to their objective of the destruction of Israel and to their terrorist means, the architects of Oslo argued that this could not happen because the Palestinians 'know only too well' that such conduct would result in the reoccupation of their cities and bring destruction on their society. What Israelis have learned since September 2000 is that not only the Palestinian leadership and elites but also the Palestinian *people* are prepared to mortgage their own future by condoning, even glorifying, these irresponsible practices. They are willing to perpetuate and intensify their own suffering if it means inflicting pain on Israel rather than seeking a compromise beneficial to both sides.

In summer 2003, when these catastrophic *domestic* consequences of terrorism for Palestinian society were already evident, another chance to break out of this vicious circle was missed. Although the government under Abu Mazen's premiership was formed on the premise that resort to massive terrorism was a strategic mistake, Abu Mazen could not produce anything more than a temporary suspension of most acts of terrorism, which would have allowed the terrorists to recuperate from the blows Israel had dealt them and to prepare for the next round. Either he could not seriously consider or he could not deliver the option of dismantling the terrorist organizations, even though that would have immediately opened the way for the speedy establishment of a Palestinian state as a result of massive international (most notably American) pressure on Israel.

The insurmountable impediment to dismantling the terrorist infrastructures, far beyond Arafat's opposition, came from the Palestinian people. There was no popular support for the abandonment of terrorism, even when just a serious *beginning* of the dismantling process could have resulted in an exit of Israeli forces from the Palestinian population centres and the removal of an array of Israeli restrictions, and could eventually have led to the establishment of a Palestinian state with provisional boundaries.

In that sense, and in that sense only, the Palestinian warning against 'civil war' was real. The few thousand active members of the terrorist organizations themselves, Hamas, Islamic Jihad and the al-Aqsa Martyrs Brigades, could not present a major problem for the tens-of-thousands-strong Palestinian security organizations. But an attempt to crack down on them was never made, even in the Gaza Strip, where these security organizations had been left largely intact. Such a crackdown could indeed have caused a civil war, because it was considered illegitimate by mainstream Palestinians.

Israeli conclusions

What all this amounts to, from an Israeli perspective, is the realization that a deal with the Palestinians is not a viable option at this time and that even an unexpected change of leadership may not bring a fundamental shift. If the Palestinian *people* endorses the rejection of Camp David and Taba, underwrites the war started immediately after it was offered the best deal ever, glorifies the suicide bombers who massacre Jewish civilians, and de-legitimizes the dismantling of terrorist infrastructures, then the *people* itself, and not only its political leadership, cannot be perceived as a partner for any kind of deal that mainstream Israelis could seriously consider.

Given that the Palestinians have broken the most fundamental commitments of the Oslo process, particularly the *unconditional* commitment to abstain from terrorism regardless of the circumstances, mainstream Israelis have very little trust in any future Palestinian commitments. Having repeatedly brought calamity on its own people, the Palestinian leadership is no longer expected to stick even to what is vital for the Palestinians themselves. All the elaborate excuses the Palestinians have concocted may impress Arabs, Europeans, some Americans and even some Israeli enthusiasts, but they fail to overshadow the bitter experience and profound mistrust of most Israelis. Their assumption is that the Palestinians will reject any formula that does not leave Israel vulnerable to their harm and that they will then use this vulnerability for blackmail, terror, or attempting to change the demographic composition of Israel.

Without actually resorting to this terminology, mainstream Israelis now consider the Palestinians to act on the assumption that their conflict with Israel is, in the most fundamental sense, a 'zero-sum game'. They conclude from the persistent Palestinian rejection of the Jewish nation-state that the quintessence of the Palestinian struggle, beyond shaking off the occupation and establishing a sovereign state, is building the Palestinian national future on the ruins of Israel. Those Israelis respond to this perceived reality with a determination to pursue unilateral action, even when it involves a major handover of territory to the Palestinians.

Since the mid-1990s, the Jewish majority in Israel has overwhelmingly (75–85 per cent) supported a disengagement policy *vis-à-vis* the Palestinians. This support was not eroded when Israelis realized that the erection of the fence was the ultimate in *unilateral* steps, and was fiercely opposed by the Palestinians for that reason. They were also aware, since the outline of the fence was made public in late 2003, that it excludes the vast majority of the territories occupied in 1967 and that it will eventually lead to the removal of most Israeli settlements. Only a small minority, corresponding to the 15–20 per cent hard-core left, insists that the fence should follow the 1967 Green Line; the solid majority supports a unilateral determination of its course.

The conclusion that unilateral disengagement is inevitable in spite of its shortcomings was born in the Zionist left and was adopted only reluctantly by the right-of-centre. Left-of-centre leaders and their constituency consistently called for partition and hoped that the Oslo process would lead to consensual disengagement along agreed lines. They were driven to the unilateral version when they became disenchanted with the Palestinian leadership, especially after it failed to meet the challenge of permanent status negotiations and started the war in 2000.

The right-of-centre leadership reluctantly adopted this policy only when it realized that perpetuation of any version of the status quo is no longer feasible because of domestic and external constraints. This realization converged with a very late-awakened awareness of the dangers of perpetuating unfettered Palestinian access to Israel. Although Prime Minister Sharon has pursued this policy with ever-growing determination since 2003, his right-of-centre camp is largely ambivalent, as there remains a considerable hard core of diehard rejectionists, comprising about one-third of his own Likud party. Sharon himself may have been torn between his lifelong political legacy and the requirements of his current responsibility, but he unmistakably opted in favour of the latter.

Value preferences

Unilateral disengagement reflects a very clear choice in terms of the priority to be accorded core values. *'Israel at peace'* comes bottom of the list, not because it is not important but because it is judged to be hopelessly unattainable at this historical stage and because futile attempts to prematurely secure an unrealistic version of peace have dangerously undermined all other values. The paramount significance of peace to Israel turned the incontrovertible ability of the Palestinians to deny it into their ultimate weapon. By taking a unilateral approach, Israel seeks to deprive them of this weapon.

Next to peace, from the bottom up, is *'The Land of Israel'*. Whereas the Jews have unquestionable historical rights to their ancestral homeland, the full exercise of these rights under the current historical and demographic circumstances would produce a state that is either not Jewish or not democratic, hence not viable (and certainly, not strong and secure).

The three top-priority values, a *'Jewish'*, *'democratic'*

113

and 'secure' Israel, are thus intimately interrelated. 'Jewish' and 'democratic' are inherently inseparable, not only because they are equally vital but also because they cannot exist separately: a state that is not democratic will in time cease to be Jewish because most Jews will not live in such a state. A Middle Eastern state that is not Jewish will soon become Arab and will be as democratic as the rest of the Arab states. The kind of Jews who made Israel into a modern, strong, successful and secure state that can survive in the harsh environment of the Middle East will unleash their talent and energy in Israel and defend it only if it is both Jewish and democratic.

The assumption of proponents of unilateral disengagement is that both the pursuit of the kind of 'peace' that the Palestinians are offering and the status quo of integration with the Palestinians in the same entity preclude a Jewish, democratic, strong and secure Israel. Compared to the clear *contradiction* between these options, there is only a manageable *tension* between the democratic and the Jewish components of the Israeli system. A tension of this kind, between personal freedoms and the requirements of public and national security, has been successfully managed for generations in every democratic nation-state.

The role of the other major parties

The Palestinians

A viable settlement ('deal') with the Palestinians, be it permanent or interim, is not a realistic option, owing to the unbridgeable gap between the hard-core positions of the parties. Even if an agreement is reached, Israelis are overwhelmingly convinced that the Palestinians will not live up to their commitments, because they are either unwilling or unable to do so, and the replacement of Arafat by Abu Mazen has not significantly eroded this conviction.

The American position

The United States cannot openly admit that final status negotiations are no longer a realistic option at this stage, but it recognizes that the real choice is between deadlock and unilateral Israeli steps. President Bush not only commended the Israeli policy as a historical opportunity but also rewarded Prime Minister Sharon with an unprecedented statement on the two major outstanding issues, borders and refugees. Although the United States remains ultimately committed to a negotiated Palestinian state, the president condoned the unilateral nature of the Israeli initiative and even promised to defend it against hostile (that is, European and UN) disruptions. The solid American backing (and Sharon's determination) have convinced Europe, Egypt and Jordan to adjust their policies to the assumption that unilateral disengagement will get under way.

Europe

Having failed to derail the Israeli strategy from the outset, the EU is determined to fit the Israeli withdrawal into the Road Map as merely the first step in that European-sponsored mechanism. *Prima facie,* this seems to be a practical approach, because Israel, like the Palestinian Authority, has accepted the Road Map and the United States (particularly the Department of State) stresses that it is still the only legitimate framework for a negotiated settlement. In practice, however, movement in accordance with the Road Map is highly unlikely: the Palestinian Authority is unable, even if it were willing, to implement the first step of dismantling the terrorist infrastructure; Israel has no motivation to entrust its most vital interests to the unfriendly or hostile members of the Quartet; and the United States has no intention of forcing it to do so. The EU may hope that whatever the outcome, the Israeli–American strategy will produce something that can be called 'implementation of the Road Map', even if the Quartet does not mould the Israeli–Palestinian reality. But although Brussels may show somewhere in the credits, the draft script is written in Jerusalem and later edited in Washington.

The Arab involvement

Egypt and Jordan are the only Arab states that could have a limited effect on Israel's disengagement, provided their role is compatible with the essentially unilateral nature of that strategy. Egypt may negotiate with Abu Mazen, as it did with Arafat, and even extract relatively minor concessions, but Israel can pursue a desirable political and security reality in Gaza regardless of the outcome of Egyptian involvement. If Egypt can deliver suppression of Palestinian terrorism without an Israeli presence, Israel will be rid of the Gaza Strip and can concentrate on the settlement blocks in the West Bank.

Should Egypt's involvement fail, Israel can re-establish its control, with the American understanding that Egypt is responsible for the failure. A major Jordanian role in the West Bank is much less likely. If it materializes, Israel can only benefit from the introduction of a responsible and dependable partner.

Unless Israel commits a major mistake that allows the Palestinians to make the Israeli–Egyptian peace treaty hostage to their national struggle, the Palestinian Authority will be trapped in a lose-lose situation: should the Arab involvement fail, the Palestinians will be left to confront Israel and the US, armed only with ineffective European sympathy; should the Jordanians and the Egyptians assume a major role, the Palestinian loss may be much more profound. The ultimate Palestinian night-mare is Israeli–Arab negotiations determining the fate of the Palestinian people and bypassing its national leader-ship. The current risk is the recurrence of the 1947–9 pattern: a blatantly unrealistic Palestinian national strategy invoking Arab involvement 'to save the Palestin-ians' but resulting in the loss of self-determination.

Urgency

Sharon has committed Israel to a time-frame by which the first major step, evacuation of the Gaza Strip, will be concluded by the end of 2005. Allowing for domestic hurdles and the impact of terrorism, this can be extended into 2006. By then, the barrier in the West Bank should be completed, indicating the extent of long-term Israeli control.

Failure to 'deliver' Gaza (full implementation) and considerable portions of the West Bank (including an initial evacuation of settlements) will have far-reaching consequences at the domestic, regional and global levels. *Domestically*, it will reflect and institutionalize a structural political deadlock, indicating that no party or coalition of parties can pursue a coherent policy that enjoys the support of the mainstream Jewish majority. Should this materialize, Israel's choice could be limited to either political paralysis or existential national decisions carried by extremely narrow margins and thus with questionable legitimacy. Indecision being a *de facto* decision for the status quo or external coercion, the legitimacy question arises anyway and all but precludes a broad-based consensus and persistent national resilience.

On the *regional* level, a major delay in disengagement will be perceived by the Palestinians and by radical Arabs as an indication of Israel's inability to proceed with its chosen strategy, at long last producing the desired effect of the protracted terror campaign: undermining Israel's two main pillars, domestic resilience and American support.

On the *global* level, a major delay would encourage unfriendly European and other initiatives designed to induce American coercion 'to break the deadlock'. Even the friendliest US administration will not shield Israel from such initiatives if it fails to offer an acceptable and workable alternative. These three levels, the domestic, the regional and the global, are intimately interrelated, complementing each other's effect not only in strengthening Israel's posture when effective policies are pursued but also in severely eroding its bargaining position if it misses the opportune moment.

Major benefits

Maintaining a Jewish and democratic nation-state

As Israel cannot, in the long run, maintain both its Jewish and democratic nature without disengaging from the Palestinians, and as a negotiated disengagement is out of the question, the essential and vital benefit of unilateral disengagement for the mainstream Jewish population is nothing less than the continued existence of the Jewish nation-state.

The underlying fear that has prompted the Jewish majority to support unilateral disengagement is the spectre of a binational Jewish–Arab entity, which would destroy the most important accomplishment of the Jewish people in the modern era, the Jewish nation-state of Israel. The fear is that if Israel continues to control the occupied territories, the Palestinians will become a majority and a *de facto* binational state will come into being, which would inevitably be transformed into an Arab state. This fear reflects the views of a cross-section of Jews in Israel – left, right and centre, religious and secular alike.

Unilateral disengagement is imperative in order to prevent the unfettered access to Israel of hundreds of thousands of Palestinians who could otherwise take up permanent residence and obtain Israeli citizenship, legally or illegally (primarily through marriage to Arab citizens of Israel). Unrestrained access to Israel has apparently already increased its Arab population by about 10–15 per cent.

For more than a century, the Arab–Israeli conflict has been waged on the demographic battlefield. The major Palestinian instrument for undermining the existence of Israel is the so-called Right of Return, which would make the Jews a minority in their own nation-state. As Israel can reject this demand and prevent its implementation, the next-best instrument for the Palestinians, if they are to reach the same objective, is a 'creeping return'. This would gradually increase the Arab minority in Israel, which already supports the Palestinian demands and largely rejects the legitimacy of the Jewish nation-state.

An effective means against Palestinian terrorism

Whereas the most *important* reason for disengagement and the fence is demographic, the most *pressing* need and rationale for this policy is the curtailment of Palestinian terrorism. The assumption here is that if the Palestinians *can* terrorize the Jewish civilian population, they *will*, regardless of negotiations or agreements. The focus of the Israeli attempt should therefore be to deny them the ability to do so rather than to convince them to refrain from trying.

The most immediate benefit of the erection of the barrier is expected to be a sharp decrease in civilian casualties owing to Palestinian suicide bombings. Although less than one per cent of terrorist actions are suicide bombings, they account for almost half of Israel's fatalities and the majority of civilian fatalities. The fence is perceived as the most effective means to prevent Palestinian terrorists from entering Israel. Only a small minority of Israeli Jews believe that it can completely eliminate terror, while a solid majority believe that the fence can diminish it considerably. The record since the erection of the fence in the northern section clearly bears out the expectations of the majority.

Securing Israel's quality of life and standard of living

Bitter experience, particularly in the 1990s, has convinced the Jews of Israel that not only their lives and nation-state are in danger if the Palestinians have unfettered access to Israel but also their quality of life and standard of living. This is not because the Palestinians are non-Jews or because they are poor. In the 1990s, Israel welcomed and absorbed hundreds of thousands of non-Jews, who came with their Jewish relatives as part of the massive immigration from the former Soviet Union. It also took in tens of thousands of some of the poorest people on earth, most of whom, before their departure from Ethiopia, had only a remote affiliation to Jewish life and the Jewish people. It is because so many Palestinians who had free access to Israel used it for terrorism and crime, killing and wounding thousands of Jews (and dozens of Arabs), forcing the Israelis to dramatically change their lifestyle, causing a major economic crisis, raising the level of criminal activity to unprecedented levels and presenting the Jewish nation-state with a major demographic threat.

121

Minimizing economic damage

Palestinian terrorism harmed the Israeli economy through direct physical damage and through the enormous expense of securing every mall, cafe, pizzeria, bus and discothèque. It devastated the tourist industry and also produced a deep and long recession (conservative estimates mention an accumulated loss of about $5 billion). This, in turn, produced major social problems when the sagging economy could no longer support the advanced welfare system. No matter how much the fence costs to build and maintain, what Israel will save in a few years of increased productivity and prevention of crime will cover its costs for many years to come.

Curbing crime

The combination of unfettered access to Israel and areas under Palestinian control produced after the Oslo Accord in essence created a perfect environment for Palestinian criminals, unrestrained by either their own population or the Palestinian Authority, on the one hand, and a nightmare for Israeli citizens and law-enforcement agencies, on the other. Palestinian criminal activity in Israel became extremely easy and rewarding when stolen goods needed to be moved only a few hundred yards or, at most, a few kilometres, to enjoy the sanctuary of the local population and a 'police' force that turned a blind eye or even collaborated with the thieves for a cut of their loot. One reliable estimate in the late 1990s attributed some 40 per cent of property crimes perpetrated in Israel to Palestinians. Car theft alone cost Israel some $300 million a year in the mid-1990s. The Palestinian 'police' drove cars stolen from Israel; the Palestinian Authority issued, for a fee, special permits for their use in the Gaza Strip and even suggested that Israel should pay a ransom to the Palestinian 'Preventive Security' agency to get some of the stolen cars back. This Palestinian crime, ignored or abetted by the Palestinian Authority and made possible by free access to Israel, considerably damaged the quality of life of Israelis and cost billions to both the state and individual citizens.

Curbing corruption

Free Palestinian access had a corrosive effect on the quality of life in Israel in a less conspicuous and direct, but no less harmful, way. The all-encompassing corruption of the Palestinian system crept into Israel and much reinforced already existing pockets of corruption in Israeli society itself. Illegal and corrupt practices that were contained in Israel thanks to the independent and corruption-free legal system, a free and prying media and a less impressive but still well-functioning police force became accessible and often untraceable following the intimate association of Israel with the Palestinian system.

Major costs

The costs of unilateral disengagement are high and painful, but mainstream Israelis seem to have realized that the costs of a perpetuated engagement with the Palestinians are prohibitive and potentially terminal for the Jewish nation-state. They compare the heavy but bearable historical, military and political costs to the catastrophic costs of a binational reality, terrorism, creeping 'return', crime and corruption.

Compromising of historical heritage, security and economy

The most important elements of the price mainstream Israelis are willing to pay are abandonment of the bulk of their historical homeland in Judea and Samaria, the dismantling of most of the settlements they have built in the populated heartland of this region, and acceptance of the major security risk of surrendering the elevated land overlooking the tiny Jewish state to a radical, belligerent, hostile and irresponsible national movement. Another major cost is the expected rift in Israeli society caused by the uprooting of settlers from beyond the fence. There is also the enormous expense of erecting the fence, maintaining and guarding it, and relocating the people living beyond it.

Most of these costs relate to partition in general, not specifically to the *unilateral* version, and have been thoroughly discussed since 1967. Most Jews do not count *the one-sided nature* of the Israeli concessions as a major cost, on the assumption that the Palestinians would not have lived up to their commitments anyway had Israel made these concessions in the framework of a reciprocal agreement.

International criticism and condemnation

The other important cost of unilateral disengagement is severe international criticism, regardless of the magnitude or risk of Israeli concessions. With the exception of the United States and a few others, the outside world is constantly criticizing and condemning Israel. The most serious problem arises in the west European democracies.

A very large portion of this criticism has little to do with any *specific* Israeli policy, and it mutates to adjust to any current issue. It is not only the mainstream in the Arab world that has adopted a thinly veiled anti-Semitic attitude towards Israel; the UN and its agencies have followed closely behind. Even in Europe, the overall picture is bleak despite the fact that Israel still has some devoted if critical friends. Some Europeans, no longer confined to the fascist right or leftist lunatic fringe, oppose disengagement (and any other Israeli policy) because it threatens to deprive them of the opportunity to blame the Jewish state for daily crimes against humanity (as well as for Palestinian inadequacies, failures and transgressions). Instead of blaming Israel for its imposed *presence* among the Palestinians, they now actually blame it for its anticipated *absence*, for 'abandoning its responsibility' and 'embracing apartheid' by disengaging from the Palestinians.

The blatant bias of the 'international community' is reflected in the blanket condemnation of Israel by the International Court of Justice in July 2004. Outlawing Israel's security fence (the 'wall'), the court ruled (para. 139) that Israel could not invoke the universally accepted 'inherent right of self-defence' when combating Palestinian terrorism because the armed attacks against Israeli citizens do not originate in a state. All 25 European states unanimously voted for a UN General Assembly resolution (21 July) adopting the court's decision, regardless of the incompatibility of this judgment concerning Israel's self-defence with the letter and spirit of the UN Charter (Article 51) and specific Security Council resolutions (1368 and 1373) adopted in 2001. Europe no longer pretends to offer even-handed consensual mediation. The High Representative for European Common Foreign and Security Policy, Javier Solana, responded to Israel's outrage at European one-sidedness by insisting that 'We will be involved whether you like it or not; you cannot prevent us respecting the rulings of the [International] Court and the [UN General] Assembly.'

The distorted image of Israel in Europe can no longer be explained away exclusively or even primarily by Israeli transgressions and public relations incompetence or by journalistic ignorance and shallow public perceptions. Israel will be condemned in Europe anyway unless it gives the Palestinians the essence of what they want, gets nothing of real substance in return and puts the Europeans in charge of the whole process. Even this will satisfy many Europeans only for a short while. The next phase is already becoming clear: questioning the very legitimacy of the *Jewish* nation-state while passionately advocating the establishment of an *Arab* Palestinian nation-state so as to partition the disputed land between two states – one that is Arab and the other that is *not* Jewish.

Paradoxically, the European response makes the Israeli decision for unilateral disengagement easier. Because criticism and condemnation are often to be expected regardless of what Israel does, it might as well get the

126

goods while it is paying the price. This situation has reached a point where international condemnation and criticism, except by America, can no longer be a major consideration of policy where the vital needs of Israel hang in the balance.

Conclusion

The inevitability of unilateral disengagement

Unilateral Israeli disengagement seems, at this point, not just possible and feasible but, judging by the mood of mainstream Israelis, almost inevitable.

The *status quo* has lost most of its constituency inside Israel, and never had one outside it. It lost its most prominent leader when Ariel Sharon espoused unilateral disengagement. The majority in the Likud's central committee, and even the party's registered members, may support this option but they do not represent the Likud electorate, let alone the mainstream Jewish vote. Any attempt to stick to the status quo under the new circumstances created by Sharon's latest statements will provoke a major rift in Israeli society and even in the Israel Defense Force. Rearguard resistance may be glorious for the diehard believers and painful for the mainstream but the outcome is obvious.

The *'peace' option* (a negotiated permanent settlement) is even more discredited. It would take nothing less than a political miracle to convince mainstream Jews in Israel that the Palestinian leadership, even with Abu Mazen at the helm, is a partner for peace willing and able to abandon terrorism, renounce the Right of Return and accept a compromise deal. And at this stage, it is extremely difficult to imagine how any amount of European funding or sponsorship could produce a mega-gimmick convincing enough to persuade Jews, except in the hard-core left, to consider a refurbished version of the Oslo act of faith after that failed so miserably.

Interim agreements and conflict management may have been a realistic starting point before the major changes that have come about recently in both Palestinian and Israeli societies. They may still constitute a useful slogan to obscure the unilateral nature of Israel's disengagement, presenting it as a part of the Road Map; but as an option in their own right they cannot prevail. The major changes on the Palestinian side have gone beyond the dysfunction of the Palestinian Authority, and include a disintegration of Palestinian political society itself. Not only is there no Palestinian leadership willing and able to deliver an end to terrorism (let alone an interim accommodation) but in the chaos that prevails there may also no longer be an organized social structure that can support such a decision.

International intervention is also not a real option, because no one is both willing and able either to coerce or to tempt the parties into a settlement. Had Israel and the Palestinians had common ground, they could have been assisted by outside powers, but such common ground does not exist. The *Palestinians* want Israel to be coerced, but the UN and Europe do not have the clout to do so and the United States does not have the motivation. *Israel* wants only one kind of input: American involvement, not as an alternative option but as support for its unilateral strategy.

Part of the strength of unilateral disengagement is that for all other policy options (regardless of whether or not their proponents admit it), it is the preferred fallback position. Should supporters of the *status quo* fail to secure their objective and be forced into partition, they would surely prefer Israel to determine its borders unilaterally, assuming that an agreement with the Palestinians or international involvement will offer Israel much less.

Israeli proponents of the *'peace' option* profess to be concerned, first and foremost, with a protracted Israeli occupation and its dangers to the Jewish and democratic nature of Israel. Should permanent status negotiations prove to be impossible or fail, they would surely prefer a unilateral exodus from the overwhelming majority of the territories and the dismantlement of most settlements over the status quo. Only an imposed peace may appeal more to the radical proponents of this option, but the only power that could seriously attempt it (the United States) is not interested.

Should the supporters of *interim agreements* come to the conclusion that there is no Palestinian partner even for a limited deal, they must prefer steps that would unilaterally produce the interim reality they want to create by agreement rather than any of the other alternatives. They must face the reality that if an interim agreement is impossible, permanent status negotiations, with or without international intervention, are completely out of the question. After all, they opted for interim agreements in the first place because they came to the conclusion that the status quo cannot and should not be perpetuated.

Should advocates of *international intervention* come to the conclusion that external powers cannot play a major role in bringing about an Israeli–Palestinian settlement, they will probably fall back on unilateral disengagement. They would not have opted for international intervention if they had considered the status quo to be desirable or bilateral attempts to reach a permanent or interim settlement to be feasible.

But for the unilateralists, there is no fall-back position. They opted for unilateralism in the first place because they despaired of all the other options. Unilateral disengagement can be unilaterally implemented and must produce at least some of the expected results. It may not deliver all the benefits and it may entail somewhat higher costs than expected, but it will certainly deprive the Palestinians of the major instruments that have enabled them to have a destructive effect on Israel. When unilateral disengagement is implemented, a new reality will emerge in which other options, hitherto unrealistic (including interim agreements), may become feasible.

Of course, unilateral disengagement should not be confused with a 'solution' to the conflict with the Palestinians or to the problems of the Jewish nation-state in the hostile Arab environment. The Middle East has long been, and remains, a bad neighbourhood. Survival in this environment sometimes calls for high fences.

6 CONCLUSIONS

Mark A. Heller

In early June 2004, the Israeli cabinet approved a plan to prepare for a four-stage disengagement and withdrawal of Israeli settlements from the Gaza Strip and the northern West Bank, to be completed by the end of 2005. This was a revised version of a plan originally submitted for consideration a month earlier, and Prime Minister Ariel Sharon was able to secure its approval and subsequent ratification in the Knesset only by removing any provisions for automatic implementation and by dismissing two of the most hardline ministers from the National Union Party.[1]

But Sharon paid a price for his partial triumph. He lost his parliamentary majority, and the ongoing revolt in his own Likud parliamentary faction and central committee complicated efforts to put together an alternative coalition that would ensure steady implementation of the plan despite increasingly vigorous extra-parliamentary opposition by the settlers and their supporters. Thus, despite continuing evidence of majority support in the general public for the disengagement and the subsequent recruitment of the Labour Party into the coalition, there is no certainty even in early 2005 that he

---

[1] In a concession to opponents in Sharon's cabinet and party, the revised plan stipulated that the actual evacuation of settlements in each stage must still be discussed and decided separately by the government.

will be able to carry it out. Furthermore, the plan, even in its original form, falls far short of the more sweeping withdrawal from major portions of the West Bank that many adherents of unilateral disengagement – represented in this volume by Dan Shueftan – have advocated as a viable, long-term conflict management measure.

In short, the protracted Israeli debate about the future of the West Bank and Gaza and of relations with the Palestinians is far from decided. This debate has preoccupied Israel and practically defined its political agenda since the Israel Defense Forces took control of those territories in the course of the Six-Day War of 1967. However, some of the central themes and assumptions in the debate have changed in important ways over the years. For example, the inevitability/desirability of a Palestinian state, a marginal issue for at least a decade after 1967, has since moved to centre stage, while what used to be known as 'the Jordanian option' – negotiating an agreement with Jordan for the return of parts of the West Bank to its control – has practically disappeared. But one constant remains: the inability of the Israeli political system to generate a consistent and coherent policy that has a reasonable chance of improving Israel's ability to address its political and security needs and to advance its goals and values more effectively, either by securing Palestinian/Arab agreement or in the absence of an agreement.

The possibility that such a policy simply does not exist cannot be categorically excluded. But assuming, for the sake of argument, that it does, the inability of the Israeli system to produce it can stem from several causes.

One is the proportional representation system of elections, which virtually precludes a one-party majority and generally leaves coalition partners united in their desire to gain and retain office but too divided on everything else to make decisive choices about critical issues. Another is the fact that for all its centrality, the Palestinian issue is not the only, and sometimes not even the primary, issue in Israeli public life. Thus, there is hardly ever a time when that issue receives the undivided attention of the political system, and there is never a 'single-issue' election that can be interpreted as unambiguous evidence of what the public really thinks about it.

But the most important reason is almost certainly the complexity and emotional intensity of the issue itself and therefore the ambivalence felt by most Israelis of almost every school of thought about every policy proposed to address it. This is evident from the chapters in this volume, whose purpose is not just to map the Israeli policy debate but to delve into the assumptions and motivations underlying the different policies advocated in that debate. These chapters articulate, *grosso modo*, the major schools of political thought. What emerges is a picture of a public divided along several axes.

The first of these axes has to do with the feasibility of peace. In a sense, this can also be defined as the axis of Israeli perceptions of Palestinian trustworthiness. The notion that movement away from the current stalemate is stymied by the loss of mutual trust is often advanced by outside analysts and sometimes even by the protagonists themselves. And although there is certainly no lack of evidence to support the assertion that neither side trusts the other, the kind of symmetry implied in this formulation is somewhat misleading. In practice, there is asymmetry in the contributions expected from the two sides in facilitating a peace agreement. Israel is expected to make concrete, material concessions; the Palestinians, in return, are expected to provide promises to sustain a peaceful relationship over the long term. Quite clearly, what influences the willingness of Israelis to make these concessions is not the extent of Palestinian trust in Israeli intentions but only the credibility of Palestinian promises of future good behaviour in the aftermath of Israeli concessions.

At the risk of oversimplification, it can be said that the advocates of 'unilateral disengagement' (represented here by Schueftan) and of 'status quo' (Harel) exhibit practically no faith at all in Palestinian trustworthiness. By contrast, the 'permanent status agreement', 'interim agreement', and 'international force' advocates (represented by Kimche, Arad and Peters and Gal respectively) show slightly greater trust – a degree of trust that can be complemented by other measures in order to reach the threshold of trust needed to make their preferences feasible. For the advocates of a permanent status agreement, this involves a modest international monitoring mechanism; for those proposing an 'international force', it involves a large and intrusive foreign presence; and for those insisting on the need for 'interim agreements', it means a phased process of relying on confidence-building measures and verification in order to provide an incremental build-up of trust over time.

What complicates this classification, however, is the fact that even those with similar evaluations of Palestinian trustworthiness can come to opposite policy conclusions, as is the case with the 'unilateral disengagement' and 'status quo' schools of thought. For the former, the question of Palestinian trustworthiness has become so hypothetical that they dismiss it from their calculation entirely and focus instead on a strategy of entrenchment in order to minimize the Palestinians' capability to harm Israel. The lack of a Palestinian 'quid' in return for the proposed Israeli 'quo' of unilaterally defined withdrawal is regarded as being of no consequence, because any 'quid' is assumed to be worthless anyway, and thus there is no point in trying to elicit one by agreeing to an even more extensive 'quo'. For the latter ('status quo'), Palestinian trustworthiness is irrelevant because even if there were trust in the credibility of a Palestinian commitment to peace, the concessions needed to secure that commitment would entail the sacrifice of a value greater than peace itself. The price is simply too high.

This difference points to a second major axis of division: the ultimate purposes or ends of policy concerning the Palestinians and the territories. Much of the Israeli debate is dominated, at least superficially, by arguments about instrumentalities or means to promote seemingly shared ends, especially security. Such arguments certainly inform the controversy over unilateral disengagement, for example, and they are marshalled in support of one position or the other. Critics charge that it will be perceived as a retreat in the face of terrorism, which will encourage even more of the same and therefore will make Israelis less secure. Advocates insist that it will reduce opportunities for terrorists to reach their targets and therefore will make Israelis more secure. By the same token, advocates of political re-engagement with the Palestinians all subscribe to the notion that a peace agreement must ultimately entail the establishment of an independent Palestinian state in virtually all the West Bank and Gaza, with its capital in Jerusalem. But they differ about whether that is also a sufficient condition for agreement – that is, if the situation is 'ripe for resolution', and, if not, what other conditions are needed (especially resolution of the refugee issue) and how much time is necessary in order to create 'ripeness'.

It is not uncommon for societies to conduct serious, even heated, political debates about alternative means to shared ends. And there is a widespread desire among Israelis to believe that the debate is 'only' about means, because that sustains hope in the possibility of maintaining or restoring national unity. But in addition to differences about means, there is an implicit division – which this volume helps to make explicit – about goals and values, or at least about the priorities assigned to common goals and values. As a result, advocates of different policies assign different, even contradictory, emphases to the same factors in the overall policy calculus. For example, people in one school of thought see territory as a critical security asset but others see it, if not as a liability, then at least as something far less important than, say, demography. And people with one frame of mind see time working to Israel's advantage but others see it as working to Israel's detriment. These divisions are very profound: notwithstanding denials to the contrary, they actually go to the very heart of visions of what Israel should be. Consequently, the aspiration to reach a consensus on this issue is very unrealistic.

However, both the political leadership and society as a whole have apparently concluded that real policy choices must await the emergence of a consensus and that no clear decisions should be made merely on the basis of a bare working majority. Perhaps this is a consequence of the political and personal fate of Yitzhak Rabin, who was the first prime minister since Ben Gurion to embark on a radical policy shift without a national consensus. The Oslo experience has discouraged the search for other breakthroughs, and the aftermath of Ehud Barak's failure to achieve one in 2000 has further reinforced the reluctance to try again.

What this seems to portend for the future is 'more of the same' – more drift, more indecision, no apocalyptic developments but also no fundamental shift away from the pattern of political, economic and security fluctuations within a fairly narrow range of familiar realities.

The question that naturally arises is whether anything can change this. There are at least three potential sources of change. The first is the disengagement proposal already approved by the Israeli government in the Sharon Plan. This proposal currently dominates the Israeli debate, largely by default. It is the major focus of political discussion and action, not only because it is pushed by the prime minister, but also because there is no real competition in the marketplace of ideas. It has provoked apprehension and opposition among Palestinians and other Arabs because it is linked to the erection of the security barrier and because it is suspected of betraying longer-term intentions about those parts of the West Bank not designated for evacuation. In the rest of the world, as in Israel itself, it has provoked responses ranging from confusion and ambivalence to varying degrees of support.

But the significant point about the reaction inside Israel is the support by those who do not share Sharon's world-view or presumed purposes and do not believe that disengagement will, by itself, suffice to bring about a significant transformation in Israel's political/security condition. Instead, those supporters believe that even a limited and modest disengagement will precipitate a dynamic that leads to developments more in keeping with their own analysis of what needs to be done. Even in this volume, it appears that advocates both of 'interim agreements' and of 'international force' can accommodate the Sharon Plan as a precursor or first stage of what they propose. And it could clearly serve as the pilot plan for the extensive unilateral disengagement outlined here. Surely it is significant too that remnants of the 'peace camp' in Israel, including even some members of the group that produced the Geneva Accord, have come out in support of Sharon, in the belief that his proposal will facilitate movement towards the permanent status agreement they endorse. If limited disengagement goes forward and they are right, then it will produce a new reality that will change the situation on the ground and thus the political constellation inside Israel – perhaps

138

enough to create if not a consensus at least a solid majority for a more decisive policy choice.

The second possible source of change is a shift in the distribution of goals and values in Israel. It is difficult to point to a specific source of such a change. If it happens at all, it will probably stem from the cumulative effect of evolving assessments of the impact of time, demography, terror, international diplomatic considerations and of the changing range of viable alternatives. Goals and values are normally slow to respond to such factors, but they are not totally unresponsive to them. The most graphic evidence is the behaviour of Ariel Sharon himself and, perhaps even more, of his deputy prime minister, Ehud Olmert. Both were identified for many decades with the uncompromising wing of the Israeli right, categorically opposed to any territorial concessions not just because attachment to the Land of Israel was a supreme value but because they argued that territory provided the best guarantee of security. In recent years, however, they have changed. Both now advocate unilateral withdrawal and the dismantling of settlements – Olmert even more than Sharon – and both now endorse what they once considered to be heresy: the establishment of a Palestinian state. These are policy shifts that stem from their responses to changing realities but also from changes in the priorities they themselves assign to competing values. And if it can happen to them, it can happen to others. Of course, it is true as well that there can be changes in the other direction, that those who once assigned a higher priority to peace can attribute less importance to it because of disillusionment with the chances of attaining it – as has happened in recent years.

This is related to a third possible source of change: a shift in Israeli perceptions of Palestinian trustworthiness stemming from changes in the actions of the Palestinians, the messages communicated by them or the character of their political leadership. There are clearly many Palestinians who are aware of the significance of their contribution to the Israeli debate, and there are some who have acted with the purpose of influencing Israeli attitudes in the direction of greater confidence in Palestinian intentions. The Geneva Accord is one such example; the Ayalon-Nusseibeh Initiative is another. It is difficult to assess the precise impact that such initiatives have already had. It is not even certain, notwithstanding the claims of its architects, that it was the publicity surrounding the Geneva Accord rather than the need to do something more dramatic about terrorism that forced Prime Minister Sharon to formulate his unilateral disengagement proposal. But whatever the effect of such actions, they have clearly not neutralized the negative impact of four years of ongoing violence, much less produced a shift towards favourable perceptions of Palestinian trustworthiness weighty enough to generate a critical change in the domestic debate about Israeli policy alternatives. To assess the probability of that happening, it will be necessary to witness a similar debate among Palestinians about their policy alternatives. Perhaps with the passing of Yasir Arafat from the Palestinian political scene, that will now become possible.

APPENDIX: MAPS

MAP 1: THE MANDATE FOR PALESTINE (IN EFFECT 1923–1948)

Beirut
THE LEBANON
Damascus
SYRIA
IRAQ
Golan Heights
Haifa
Jenin
Nablus
Tel Aviv
Jaffa
Jerusalem
Gaza
PALESTINE
Negev Desert
Jordan River
Amman
Dead Sea
Kerak
TRANSJORDAN
Ma'an
ARABIA
EGYPT
Aqaba

Area ceded by Great Britain to the French Mandate of Syria in 1923

Transjordan removed from the Mandate for Palestine in 1922

143

MAP 2: AREAS A, B AND C
(OSLO II AGREEMENT 1995)

Source: Foundation for Middle East Peace